A Cultural History of Madrid

A Cultural History of Madrid

Modernity and the Urban Spectacle

Deborah L. Parsons

Oxford • New York

First published in 2003 by
Berg
Editorial offices:
1st Floor, Angel Court, 81 St Clements Street, Oxford, OX4 1AW, UK
838 Broadway, Third Floor, New York, NY 10003-4812, USA

Berg is an imprint of Oxford International Publishers Ltd.

Library of Congress Cataloging-in-Publication Data
Parsons, Deborah L., 1973-
    A cultural history of Madrid : modernism and the urban spectacle /
Deborah L. Parsons.
        p. cm.
Includes bibliographical references and index.
        ISBN 1-85973-646-7 (cloth) – ISBN 1-85973-651-3 (paper)
    1. Madrid (Spain)–Civilization–20th century. 2. Popular
culture–Spain–Madrid–History–20th century. 3. Modernism
(Art)–Spain–Madrid. I. Title.
DP357.P37 2003
946'.41–dc21

                                                            2003000663

British Library Cataloguing-in-Publication Data
A catalogue record for this book is available from the British Library.

ISBN 978-1-85973-651-7 (Cloth)

Typeset by JS Typesetting Ltd, Wellingborough, Northants.
Printed in the United Kingdom by Biddles Ltd, Guildford and King's Lynn.

www.bergpublishers.com

Madrid is for me an immense book, a lively theatre, in which each day I find new pages to read, new and curious scenes to observe.

(Ramón Mesonero Romanos)

The court is a city of contrasts; it displays intense light next to dark shadow.

(Pío Baroja)

Contents

List of Illustrations

Acknowledgements

I am extremely grateful to the staff of the Museo Municipal, the Museo de la Ciudad and the Reina Sofia art gallery in Madrid, and of the Eliot-Phelips Collection at the University of London Library, for their generous help and assistance, and to the Arts and Humanities Research Board for providing the research leave funding that allowed me to bring the writing of this book to completion. There are many other people who have supported this project from its beginning to end. Firstly I would never have embarked upon this project without the consistent encouragement of Jo Labanyi and Laura Marcus, whose intellectual energy and perspicacity are always so inspirational. My colleagues in the Department of English at the University of Birmingham have as ever provided the strongest support, and I thank in particular Tony Davies, Andrzej Gasiorek and Marcus Walsh for their scholarly acumen and mentorship. Numerous friends and colleagues have shared their urban knowledge and their urban passions, among them Maria Balshaw, Helena Buffery, Jan Campbell, Graeme Gilloch, Liam Kennedy, Helen Laville, Solange Mouthaan and Steve Pile. I owe a special debt to Vicky Buffery for all her translation work, to Kathleen May for her patience and kindness as editor, and again to Maria Balshaw, whose insightful suggestions and continued encouragement have been invaluable to me. My warmest thanks also to Angela and Vicente Gasca for their affection and hospitality. This book is for David, who put up with my scribbles with amused indulgence, and who started it all by first taking me to Sol.

Abbreviations

Whenever possible, quotations from texts are taken from standard translations available to the general reader. In all other cases, translations from the original have been commissioned specifically for this volume.

B   Benito Pérez Galdós, *That Bringas Woman*, ed. and trans. Catherine Jagoe (London: Everyman, 1996)

C   Ramón Gómez de la Serna, *Cinelandia*, (Madrid: Valdemar, 1995)

D   Benito Pérez Galdós, *The Disinherited*, ed. and trans. Lester Clark (London: Phoenix House, 1976)

FJ   Benito Pérez Galdós, *Fortunata y Jacinta*, ed. and trans. Agnes Moncy Gullón (London: Penguin, 1986)

HPS   Ramón Gómez de la Serna, *Historia del Puerta del Sol* (Madrid: Almarubu, 1998)

LB   Pío Baroja, *La Busca, Obras Completas*, vol. 1 (Madrid: Biblioteca Nueva, 1948)

LBo   Ramón del Valle-Inclán, *Luces de Bohemia*, ed. and trans. Anthony Zaahareas (Edinburgh: Edinburgh University Press, 1976)

MC   José Gutiérrez Solana *Madrid callejero* (Madrid: Castalia, 1995)

MM   Ramón Mesonero Romanos, *Manual de Madrid* (Madrid: D. M. de Burgos, 1831)

OWS   Walter Benjamin, *One-Way Street and Other Writings* (London: Verso, 1979)

–1–

Introduction: The Castizo Metropolis

In 1992, less than two decades after emerging from the Fascist dictatorship of General Franco, Spain announced its cultural and specifically urban renaissance with tripartite force, hosting the Olympics in Barcelona, the World Exposition in Seville and the European City of Culture in Madrid. From the reactionary authoritarianism and stagnancy of the Franco years, Spain was suddenly the centre of the vision of an integrated European heritage, a status judiciously shared out across the representative cities of internally rivalrous cultural identities. Ten years on and Barcelona has become an icon of the 'new' Euro-urbanity and a model for Leftist policies of design-led urban regeneration. After a long history of stubborn resistance to European influence, however, Madrid retains its political hegemony but, to international eyes at least, cannot compete with the cosmopolitan style and cultural aura of the Catalan city. 'Madrid is not a city of ancient charm', declares one *Guardian* travel article, going on to recommend that it is instead 'a place whose present is generally more interesting than its past'.[1]

A cautious erasure of the political resonance of the past, and a determined emphasis on the consumerist neutrality of the present, typifies contemporary publicity of the city. It is not only Barcelona's architectural heritage and regeneration that has made it a favourite example within the urban policies of Leftist European governments. In its layout, its monuments and the imperial grandeur of much of its official architecture, Madrid bears testimony to a succession of more or less autocratic rulers and regimes; not least Philip II, who first chose the unprepossessingly positioned city as the home of the Hapsburg court in the sixteenth century. Of the most recent, however, General Francisco Franco, there is a conspicuous absence. Resisting the onslaught of the Nationalist forces until the last days of the Civil War, Madrid was nevertheless declared by Franco, following Philip before him, as the symbolic capital of his own vision of a centralised imperial regime, its local urban identity submerged under a myth of universal 'Spanishness'. Today, with the exception of a single statue, the Fascist dictator has been carefully removed from the city's official cultural memory. If the Franco years were a 'time of silence', marked by the censorship and repression of all that challenged the values of the New State, they have now themselves been silenced by the narrative of a democratic, eurocentric Spain.[2]

'Madrid is as unembraceable as a human being. As contradictory and as varied', its internationally renowned film director Pedro Almodóvar declared in 1991, evoking what is perhaps one of the city's most distinct characteristics.[3] Madrid is a city of extremes. Stranded between the flat plains of Castile and the mountain range of the Sierra Guadarrama, it can seem as contradictory as its notoriously fierce climate. If, for the idiosyncratic Almodóvar, this is part of its allure, visitors to the city have long been inclined to disagree. 'Is it to be wondered at, that this capital should be so very insalubrious?', grumbled the English traveller Richard Ford in 1846, 'In winter you are frozen alive, in summer baked'.[4] Others, frustrated by the wilderness of the mid-afternoon siesta, and the apparently stubborn lethargy of bureaucratic officials, complain of idleness and inefficiency. Those ignorant of the city's predilection for midnight revelry, however, have been caught unawares by its indefatigable nightlife and a common culture of dining well into the twilight hours. Describing his first morning in Madrid, faced with the prospect of touring an array of national monuments, churches and museums, Alain de Botton admits, 'My overwhelming wish was to remain in bed and, if possible, catch an early flight home'.[5] He resisted the temptation but confesses that, venturing out from his hotel into the Puerta del Sol, Madrid's congested central square, 'I wondered, with mounting anxiety, what I was to do here, what I was to think'.[6]

There is a plaque set in one of the paving stones of the Puerta del Sol that marks the kilometre zero of Spain, the spot from which all distances are measured. Childish delight in standing on the stone, however, quickly fades to a feeling of emptiness, even absurdity. Fifty years earlier than Botton, the travel writer H. V. Morton described Sol as 'a confusion . . . a fascination . . . a magnet', continuing, '[s]omehow you always find yourself there; if you are lost, you go there and recover your bearings'.[7] His statement captures the square's essential contradiction, its role as both the official centre of a nation and the chaotic and anarchical heart of a city and its people. The eastern entrance to Moorish Madrid, the 'Gate of the Sun' is not a place for self-reflexive contemplation; it is loud, brash and fast-moving, an eclectic mix of the city's past and present. Neither a gate nor a square, it is instead an un-geometrical semicircle. A site where the traditional and the contemporary have always combined incongruously, 'orientation' most appropriately means a tight hold on one's wallet and a sharp eye alert to the heavy stream of cars and taxis. Yet with all its ambiguities, indeed because of them, perhaps the Puerta del Sol still offers a key to Madrid after all. Confusion and fascination, produced by a constant clash of traditional local colour and sporadically energetic modernisation, characterise experience of the city throughout the nineteenth and early twentieth centuries. *A Cultural History of Madrid* introduces dreams, stories and images of its changing landscape by a variety of visitors and Madrilenians, exploring the material, mythical, symbolic and emotional maps that they produce. Taken together, these form a historical narrative of Madrid's halting and abortive transition to modernity, only fully resumed within the democratic change of the 1980s and 1990s.

Writing on Cities

Botton's enquiry highlights the ways in which the exoticising presuppositions of the traveller, and similarly the standardising theories of the critic, can suddenly become unsustainable when applied to a particular city in all its locality and immediacy. My aim with this book is thus also to invite recognition of specificity as an important element of thinking about cities. The annals of urban sociology and cultural theory have established the modern city as of central importance in the understanding of modernity, along with an accepted conceptual framework for its analysis. In classic accounts of urban modernity, the city is the site where the maelstrom of social, technological and psychological change is felt most keenly. Industrialisation, technology, consumer capitalism, unprecedented demographic growth; together these spawned a new urban entity, the metropolis, which in turn brought with it a new urban sensibility. For Georg Simmel, for example, the city concentrates and thus epitomises the conditions of modern capitalist society, identified in his seminal essay 'The Metropolis and Mental Life' (1903) as shock, indifference, neurasthenia and estrangement.[8] The speed and shocks of everyday life in the metropolis resulted in a modern urban dweller whose hypersensitive and increasingly benumbed nervous system demanded ever new and ever more intense stimulation. Metropolitan experience, according to Simmel, was thus the antithesis of traditional life in which social relations were slower, more familiar and more intimate. Equally influential has been Walter Benjamin's work on nineteenth-century Paris as the epitome of urban modernity, and his key architectural and experiential metaphors for exploring its commodified phantasmagoria; the arcades, the boulevards, the prostitute and the *flâneur*.[9]

More recently, from literary and art historical studies, Raymond Williams has pointed to the tradition of the writer as urban walker and observer in literary representations of the city. T. J. Clark's landmark study *The Painting of Modern Life*, and Christopher Prendergast's equally excellent *Paris and the Nineteenth Century*, have encouraged recognition of the visual dynamics of the cityscape, and emphasised a 'canon' of spectacular spaces that define the landscape of urban modernity, such as boulevards, theatres, parks, cafés and department stores. Feminist scholarship by Griselda Pollock and Janet Wolff, among others, has in turn illustrated the exclusion of women as observing subjects from this new city space, and their restriction to either a private, domestic sphere or to highly object-ified roles within the cityscape. Adrian Rifkin's *Street Noises*, moreover, extends these debates into the more socially marginal spaces of the café-cabaret and the fleamarket.[10] *A Cultural History of Madrid* depends on the insights of this extensive and fundamental body of urban research for an understanding of crucial elements of urban modernity, yet it also attempts to supplement them. A palpable lack of attention, in my opinion, has been paid to cities that differ from the 'norm' constituted by the (highly idiosyncratic and themselves distinct) examples of Paris, London and New York. While it is certainly true that these three cities have become paradigmatic as a result of their economic and cultural pre-eminence within Western society, I would argue that it does not follow that they therefore exhaust understanding of the conditions and representation of urban modernity in all its manifold complexity. This is obviously not to suggest that accounts of the metropolitan experience based on these cities are in any way invalid, but rather to warn against the generalising theories that are too often derived from them, and the occlusion of other, contradictory or qualifying examples. Too often in contemporary criticism, as Nigel Thrift has pointedly remarked, it is assumed that 'one city tells all'.[11]

In their 1991 preface to the new edition of *Modernism, 1890–1930*, Malcolm Bradbury and James McFarlane present a tantalisingly suggestive list of what they describe as 'hidden' cities of modernism, including 'Rome, Vienna, Prague, Budapest, Munich, Berlin, Zurich, Oslo, Barcelona, Saint Petersburg, even Dublin and Trieste', most of which, it has to be said, continue to be overlooked in studies of urban modernity.[12] Madrid, seemingly unable to make the grade of even a forgotten city of modernism, is significantly absent. Given the vibrancy of its international avant-garde cultural scene throughout the first three decades of the twentieth century that are Bradbury and McFarlane's period of study, it is tempting to wonder why. 'How is Spain different and why?' has become a leading question within Hispanic cultural studies, concerned with exploring its erosion from the historiography of European modernisation. Jo Labanyi, for example, has recently suggested that Spanish culture has been constructed as a loser within the narrative of progressive, nineteenth century Europe, not only second-rate in its assimilation of modernity, but also a fading world power, a fact consolidated by the loss of its final colonies to the newly mighty USA in 1898.[13] Spain's supposed failure at modernisation, Labanyi suggests, depends on a northern European perspective that, privileging its own norms, emphasises the evolutionary ethos of capitalist development and technological experiment, along with an elite division of high and low culture, as the paradigmatic conditions of modernity. Spain does not align with the accepted periodisation, concepts and practices of modernism and modernity in this sense. Delayed industrialisation, the belated emergence of a then conservative and economically weak bourgeoisie, the loss of empire, and, in particular, neutrality during the First World War, indicate some aspects of the nation's lack of parity with the experiences of European modernity more generally.

This is not to suggest that broader European experiences of modernisation do not pertain to Madrid however. In a comparison of demographic expansion over the nineteenth century, for example, during which time London almost doubled in size and Paris more than doubled, Madrid's population tripled from 167,000 (in 1797) to 500,000 (in 1900), escalating to almost one million by 1930, much of the increase due to external migration from the provinces.[14] Verbal and visual representations of the city, moreover, engaged with the changing landscape with anxieties and fantasies of urban living similar to those evinced elsewhere in Europe, as well as the familiarly obsessive desire to objectify the city and make it knowable. Michael Ugarte's *Madrid 1900* is an excellent account of the city in this respect, drawing on key models of urban literary criticism to study the representation of the turn-of-the-century city and a new urban consciousness in the work of the writers Pío Baroja, Valle-Inclán, Azorín, Carmen de Burgos and Ramón Gómez de la Serna.[15] But, following Labanyi's argument, Madrid also gives pause to our conceptualisations of modernity, both in its paradigmatic sense as epoch, progress and rationalisation, and in its various mutations (high modernity, late modernity, postmodernity). The modernity of Madrid is ambiguous, characterised by a late but then urgent modernisation that overlapped with the persistence of traditional cultural elements and ways of life. For much of the nineteenth century its appearance was that of a town rather than a metropolis, its official status as *Villa y Corte* [Town and Court] describing it perfectly: small, crudely designed and insular in attitude, while yet the seat of a flamboyant if fading empire. Created as an 'artificial capital' that would function primarily as a court rather than a city, it never really achieved the social and economic infrastructure of its major European counterparts until the 1900s.[16] It was only in the first decades of the twentieth that modernisation began in earnest, helped by the reinvestment of capital after Spain lost its final colonies in 1898, as well as a briefly profitable export market during the First World War.

Rhythms of Modernity

What is particularly interesting about the Spanish capital is that its ineffectual aspiration to modernity throughout the nineteenth century, alongside a self-delusive pretence at imperial grandeur, presents a distorted reflection of capitalist bourgeois modernity, or as the writer Ramón María del Valle-Inclán described in 1922, 'a grotesque deformation of European civilization'.[17] Marshall Berman provides a useful context in this respect, in his argument for a 'modernism of underdevelopment'.[18] For Berman, the examples of Paris and St Petersburg illustrate an inherent binarism within the history of modernism, in which spectacular examples of industrial and economic progress constitute a norm against which other nations and cities become anomalies (and in standard narratives of modernity simply invisible):

> At one pole we can see the modernism of advanced nations, building directly on the materials of economic and political modernization and drawing vision and energy from a modernized reality – Marx's factories and railways, Baudelaire's boulevards – even when it challenges that reality in radical ways. At an opposite pole we find a modernism that arises from backwardness and underdevelopment.[19]

The issue raised here is not of a clear distinction between dynamic modernisation and stagnant tradition, between modernity and non-modernity, but of a more complex scenario in which late forms of modernity attempt to live up to the example of the leading world economies. 'The modernism of underdevelopment', Berman continues, 'is forced to build on fantasies and dreams of modernity, to nourish itself on an intimacy and a struggle with mirages and ghosts'.[20] Without equivalent means and resources, however, these visions remain hauntingly unachievable, resulting only in superficial reflections or grotesque distortions of the modernity they mimic. Madrid's attempts to imitate the larger, more productive and more economically prosperous metropoli of Paris and later New York, were indeed hesitant and largely unsuccessful. If Paris, as Walter Benjamin declares, was the supreme embodiment of nineteenth-century modernity, Madrid revealed the process to be far less smooth and absolute than Baron Haussmann's wholesale demolition job on the French capital implied. My interest, then, is in the ways in which the city corresponds to, but also *complicates* or *contradicts*, the classic approaches of urban theory and historical modernism. This book is thus not so much an attempt to integrate Madrid under the paradigms of modernist studies, as to investigate its ambiguous and uneven assimilation of modernity as this was played out across the constant imagining and reimagining of its urban landscape. It is an exploration of the ways in which Madrid is different, and an argument for acknowledging the narratives of its alternative modernity.

Revising critical assumptions about the modern city, however, requires more than simply the inclusion of previously overlooked or dismissed examples under current paradigms. It also demands fresh perspectives on the ways in which those paradigms may be challenged, as well as a reconceptualisation of our basic interpretative hypotheses and hierarchies. A current generation of urban theory has been a formative influence on my thinking in this respect. For, as what counts as a 'city' becomes increasingly ambiguous in the global, technological economy of the contemporary world, so we are forced to revise the ways in which we understand cities as spatial and historical formations.[21] I do not want to imply here that urban conditions are not historically delimited, but I do argue that the current rethinking and reimagining of the urban offers new insights into the ways in which we conceive cities in the past as much as in the present; Madrid, for example, was a 'transnational' city in the sixteenth century, indeed the capital of a transcontinental empire. 'The postmodern project', suggests David Ley, 'is the re-enchantment of the built environment', the revival of the social and cultural diversity of urban space after the universalising functionalism of modernist design, or, in the words of Henri Lefebvre, of people's 'right to the city'.[22]

Essential to the 'new urbanism' is thus an awareness of, and methodological commitment to, the interrelation of the geographical, the sociological and the aesthetic imaginations in the production and analysis of urban space. In particular, this involves the synthesis of two traditions of understanding urban experience: firstly, the 'phenomenality' of the city, or how people use urban space, and secondly, the 'urban imaginary', or how it is envisaged, represented and remembered, along with the ways in which both mediate the interplay of power and everyday life in the city.[23] Taken together, these two concerns highlight the interdependence of the material, the sensory and the psychological as a key element in the postmodern theorising of cities in all their cultural and historical complexity and diversity. For the purposes of this book, the role of this aspect of urban theory in the work of Lefebvre and Walter Benjamin provides a conceptual framework with which to explore Madrid against the standard theoretical syntax of urban modernity. The historical materialist underpinnings of both Benjamin and Lefebvre's writings imply ways of thinking about cities where the rhythms and modalities of space are outside the established norms of bourgeois modernity. Both, for example, made the city central to their spatial analyses of capitalist modernity, and both shared a commitment to the everyday as the means by which the phenomenality of modern urban life could be understood. Yet both also discovered in the spatial character of Mediterranean and Eastern European cities forms of urbanity distinct from those of Northern Europe, that would be influential for their own methodologies, but that would also be useful for highlighting urban patterns of modernity typically neglected because of their variance from the conceptual norm.

The everyday urban rhythms of a reluctantly modernising Madrid were significantly different to those of the metropolis epitomised by Simmel's Berlin. Yet despite his massive generalisation in describing Paris as *the* capital of the nineteenth century, we find in Benjamin a fascinated sensitivity towards the specific cadence and minutiae of diverse urban environments that is instructive for this study. The particularity of a city, for Benjamin, was to be found in the vernacular of its everyday life, and if the Parisian arcades famously embodied the 'mythology' of bourgeois modernity, the different spatial form and culture of other cityscapes suggested to him antithetical experiences and principles. One of the most obvious examples of this can be found in the early impressionistic essay 'Naples', the outcome of a journey that Benjamin made to Capri and Naples in the summer of 1924 with his lover Asja Lacis.[24] Naples seems to have had a stirring effect on

Benjamin, for whom the Mediterranean city's 'oriental' character and 'highly temperamental way of life' contrasted sharply with the bourgeois individualism and impersonality of the Northern European capitals of Paris and Berlin.[25] The literary sketch that he proceeded to write with Lacis, presents the city as anarchic and carnivalesque, characterised by the tactile experience of its chaotic and theatrical streets, and the porous quality of its buildings, traditions and everyday life.

'Porosity is the inexhaustible law of the life of this city, reappearing every-where' (*OWS*, 171), Benjamin declares, describing the interaction of public and private, work and play, past and present, tradition and modernity:

> Building and action interpenetrate in the courtyards, arcades, and stairways. In every-thing they preserve the scope to become a theatre of new, unforeseen constellations. The stamp of the definitive is avoided. No situation appears intended forever, no figure asserts its 'thus and not otherwise'. This is how architecture, the most binding part of the communal rhythm, comes into being here: civilized, private, and ordered only in the great hotel and warehouse buildings on the quays; anarchical, embroiled, village-like in the centre (*OWS*, 169)

The architectural form of Naples constructs the city as a communal theatre for the improvised choreographies of everyday life: 'Buildings are used as a popular stage. They are all divided into innumerable, simultaneously animated theatres. Balcony, courtyard, window, gateway, staircase, roof are at the same time stages and boxes' (*OWS*, 170). For its inhabitants, then, Naples is not a planned system (street numbers, for example, are irrelevant to most of its population, who orientate themselves by an internalised map of affect) but a constant variety show of humour and pathos. To the accompaniment of a barrel organ, street vendors trade using 'the most ancient fairground practices' (*OWS*, 173), a fat lady and a cavalier perform a ludicrous double act, and an itinerant artist draws the figure of Christ in coloured chalks on the asphalt, to be rubbed away when he has left by the constant flow of pedestrian feet.

The 'passion for improvisation' and theatrical 'porosity' that dominates the temperament of Benjamin's Naples, is a common feature in the popular repres-entation of Madrid, from the sketches of common life of nineteenth-century *costumbrismo* to the clichés of contemporary tourism. The form and pace of modernity in its most familiar, Northern European form is anomalous in Madrid, as it is in the Italian city. The department store, for example, Benjamin declares, 'in other cities the rich, magnetic centre of purchasing', is in Naples 'devoid of charm, outdone by the tightly packed multiplicity' of open street life (*OWS*, 174). Even private life is marked by porosity, 'far less the refuge into which people retreat than the inexhaustible reservoir from which they flood out' (*OWS*, 174). 'To exist',

Benjamin observes, 'for the Northern European the most private of affairs, is here
. . . a collective matter' (*OWS*, 174). If Benjamin's Parisian metaphor for the
walker-observer of the city, the *flâneur*, turns the street into his private interior, he
nevertheless remains detached in his own bounded subjective space; in Naples
people resist the very division of public and private. In the porous city such
divisions dissolve. Finding his tourist guide all but useless, Benjamin thus turns
instead to what he described as 'my inductive way of getting to know the topography of different places', in which the 'first and most important thing you have
to do is feel your way through a city'.[26] In his writing, finding the abstractions of
theory similarly irrelevant, he attempted a critical approach that would articulate
the particularity, texture and immanence of urban life. The *flâneur*, wandering
amidst the reflective glass surfaces of the arcades, at once within and yet detached
from the crowd, is a very different figure to that of the Benjamin of 1924, feeling
his way through the tactile city of Naples.

There is undoubtedly a degree of romanticisation in Benjamin's celebration of
the Mediterranean city, notably for example in his ability to describe the fascination of '[e]ven the most wretched pauper' with the colourful scene of its street life,
'enjoying in all his poverty the leisure to follow the great panorama' (*OWS*, 170).
His assertion that in Naples 'the festival penetrates each and every working day'
(*OWS*, 171), however, is not merely a precursor to the current 'festivity' beloved
of postmodern urban planning. Instead it points to the importance of recognising
the influence of the sacred, and of ritualised spatiality, as these persist within the
secular landscape of the bourgeois city. Lefebvre too recognised the perseverance
of cyclical rhythms of ritual as central to the everyday life of Southern European
cities, and the resulting coexistence of burgeoning modernisation alongside more
traditional, local features. In Mediterranean cities, he argues in a posthumously
published essay, 'historical characteristics appear to persist with extraordinary
power more than elsewhere', most obviously in their public, civic spaces which,
similar to the everyday theatricality observed by Benjamin, function as a 'vast
scene-setting' against which '[r]ituals, codes and relations become visible and
acted out'.[27]

Lefebvre's argument for the way in which such urban theatricality subverts the
role of monumental and ritualised spaces as mediums of power, is particularly
interesting here. The reflection of the authority of monarch and Church from its
origins as imperial capital, the Madrid cityscape became a fiercely contested site
over the course of the nineteenth century, as a professional bourgeois elite, liberal
government and restored monarchy all sought to mark their identity in the built
form of the city. 'Political power dominates or attempts to dominate space',
Lefebvre states, 'hence the importance of monuments and squares', which convey
particular narratives of power (*WC*, 237). Nevertheless, he continues, the meanings
of such symbolic sites can themselves be contested and manipulated in a struggle

for space 'in which rhythms play a major role', and localised social temporality 'seeks and manages to shield itself from State, linear, unirhythmical measured and measuring time' (*WC*, 237). We return here to the subversion of authoritative conceptions of rationalised space by the theatricality and porosity of the everyday, through which an organized 'space of representation, 'spontaneously' becomes a place of promenades, encounters, intrigues, diplomacy, trade and negotiations, theatricalizing itself (*WC*, 237). Although Lefebvre rather optimistically overstates the potential of improvised human encounter as a force within urban politics, his recognition of the clash between the symbolic meanings of space and the ways in which that space is actually used and lived is instructive.

Even as Madrid gradually acquired the hallmarks of a bourgeois metropolis, the city retained a resilient counter-cultural identity based in a popular mythology of its traditional working class. *Castizo* Madrid has a long heritage in the city's collective imaginary. Translatable as 'authentically Spanish', the term *castizo* was used by mid-nineteenth-century Madrid writers and commentators to describe the popular, local colour of its lower classes, and in particular the social identity of the southern-lying *barrios* [neighbourhoods] of La Latina, Lavapiés and Embajadores. Initially the outer-city settlements of the city's Jewish and Muslim population, by the seventeenth and eighteenth centuries these areas had become occupied by a growing trade and servant class. The lively street culture and reputed wit, raillery and arrogance of this social group were soon inflated into a cult identity of *majismo*, epitomised in the elegant and playful young men and women of Goya's early paintings. The stereotypical characters, *verbenas* (street parties), amusements and milieu of *majismo*, sentimentally portrayed by writers and artists and embraced by the popular imagination, persisted into the nineteenth century as *lo castizo*, a nostalgic construction of traditional *madrileño* character that was regularly depicted in the light journals and theatre of the time.

As a specifically localised identity, set firmly within the urban lifestyle of Madrid's ancient slums, *lo castizo* contrasted with both the national and imperial symbolism of the city on the hand, and its burgeoning European modernity on the other. The term was constantly appropriated and redefined by popular, intellectual and political discourse throughout the nineteenth and twentieth centuries, however, from the Liberal Romanticism of the 1830s to Franco's folkloric Fascism a century later. The ascendance of nationalism as part of the cultural production of liberal capitalism across Europe in the nineteenth century, resulted in the 'diminished importance of community on a local scale and the social significance of place along with it'.[28] Redefined by national ideologies, *lo castizo* was naturalised into the 'authentic' expression of Spanish cultural character and lost much of its specific urban context and cadence; multicultural, lower-class Madrid substituted by a fantasised rural Castile. The tension of *castizo* Madrid with both Spanish and European modernity is thus integral to narratives and images of the city, revealing the complex relation of its local, national and transnational identities as they were practised, symbolised and re-articulated across the urban landscape.[29]

How do notions of cosmopolitanism and *castizo* inform our understanding of nineteenth- and early twentieth-century Madrid? How were they played out in the spatial form of the city? In what ways were dreams of the modern and the pull of tradition juxtaposed within the cultural history of Madrid? These are thus the fundamental questions that this study pursues and explores, investigating the ambiguous relationship of these competing ideologies as they circulate within the built form, everyday life and representation of the city. To this end *A Cultural History of Madrid* diverges from Ugarte's focus on the representation of the city by the literary canon, to emphasise the interaction of a broader range of urban cultural phenomena in the highly contested configuration of the city as a lived and imagined space; yes, the journalistic vignette and the novel, but also urban planning and architecture, popular theatre and cinema. Beginning in the 1830s with the disentailment of Church and royal lands and the beginnings of a new, secular urban landscape (chapter 1), I analyse the period from the city's expansion into a bourgeois capital after the fall of the Isabeline monarchy (chapter 2), to the contradictions of society spectacle and extreme poverty under the Restoration (chapter 3), the eventual onset of metropolitan modernity at the turn of the century (chapter 4), and the technological and commercial 'Europeanization' of the first decades of the twentieth century before the trauma of civil war and repressive dictatorship (chapter 5). I trace the different visions of this changing Madrid through a variety of its chroniclers, among them the Romantic essayists Ramón Mesonero Romanos and José Mariano de Larra, the novelists Benito Pérez Galdós, Pío Baroja and Ramón de Vallé-Inclán, and the avant-gardists Ramón Gómez de la Serna and Maruja Mallo, exploring the images and metaphors with which they at once represent and shape the urban landscape and urban consciousness.

A brief epilogue considers contemporary Madrid within the context of the new urge to modernity of post-Franco Spain, focusing specifically on its depiction within the films of Pedro Almodóvar. For if in much of Western society, as Marshall Berman argues, 'we find ourselves today in the midst of a modern age that has lost touch with the roots of its own modernity', in Spain the death of Franco initiated a late twentieth-century need to look back over the gap of four decades of dictator-ship, in order to recover and reaffirm lost national, ethnic and sexual identities, at the same time as it prompted a radical break with the past and embrace of a new modernity.[30] The 'cult of the new', that Paul Julian Smith in his groundbreaking book *The Moderns* describes as the distinctive trait of contemporary urban Spain, perhaps marks the eventual maturation in Madrid of a long dormant modernist project.[31] Madrid still aspires to be 'obviously modern', Alain de Botton for example remarks, 'as though modernity were a longed-for good that one needed in extra strong doses to compensate for an earlier lack'.[32] Almodóvar has been the self-styled arbiter of this modern Madrid for over two decades, credited with defining the radical face and frivolous climate of the city during the Transition. While flaunting a radical and provocative modernity, however, parodying the folkloric myths of traditionalist Spain, his films nevertheless also rehistoricise and pay homage to Madrid's *castizo* culture. It is perhaps with this at first exaggerated, yet more recently increasingly self-reflexive representation of the co-existence of the modern and the *castizo* in the life and landscape of the city, that Almodóvar thus most appropriately defines Madrid's inimitable identity.

–2–

Madrid, 'Villa y Corte'

Under the Austrian Habsburg dynasty, Madrid was the fifth largest city in Europe and the royal court of an empire over which the sun never set. Somewhat paradoxically, however, its capital status was in part the result if its *lack* of earlier historical eminence. Originating as an Arab fortress town in the ninth century, founded to protect the nearby Toledo from Christian attack, it remained little more than a small rural town and modest trading centre throughout the medieval period, despite gradually gaining royal favour as a residential retreat. Ferdinand and Isabella preferred Valladolid for the location of their court, and their grandson Charles V, Habsburg king and Holy Roman Emperor, travelled too widely to settle in any one city. His son, Philip II, however, to whom he left the largest empire in history (including the Iberian Peninsula, Central and Southern America, Burgundy, the Netherlands, Naples, Sicily, Sardinia and the Philippines) sought a central and permanent capital.

Philip's decision to install the Habsburg court at Madrid in 1561 is generally agreed to have been both arbitrary and short-sighted. The city had no illustrious past to speak of, no grand monuments and no navigable river. What sixteenth-century Madrid did offer, however, was a suitably blank page for the writing of the king's narrative of imperial monarchy. The relative insignificance of Madrid's political and religious heritage in comparison with that of Toledo or Valladolid was ideally suited to Philip's desire for a neutral centre, and the city's geographical centrality within Spain seems to have appealed to his fascination for mathematical order. Moreover, its elevation to the status of capital would provide a clear demonstration of his absolute monarchical power. In making the provincial town the capital of an empire, Philip inscribed upon it a specific material and symbolic identity. Socially, politically, economically and topographically, Madrid had become *la Villa y Corte*, a capital by royal decree (Fig. 1).

Madrid's population rose dramatically with the arrival of the court, from about 18,000 in 1561 to over 80,000 by the end of Philip's reign in 1598, as people flooded to the city from the local provinces in search of work. An overwhelming majority were serviced to the court as servants, military, bureaucratic or religious staff, or as artisans in luxury trade, resulting in what was a predominantly floating population.[1] The consolidation of the permanency of the royal household brought with it significant urban embellishment, notably in the building of the

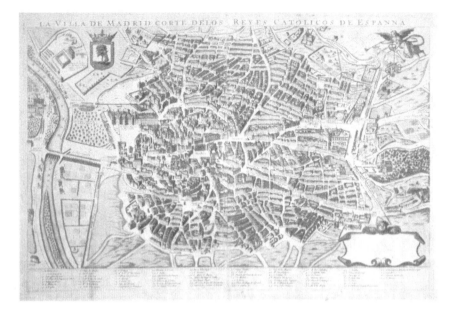

Figure 1 *La Villa de Madrid Corte de los Reyes Católicos de España* (1635), Museo Municipal de Madrid

Plaza Mayor, where state ceremonies, fiestas, bullfights and public executions were held, the development of the Puerta del Sol into the social centre of the city, and the extension of the city to the east by the establishment of the gardens and palace of the Buen Retiro. By the seventeenth century Madrid was a world capital with a vibrant cultural and artistic society. The lavish decadence of its aristocracy, however, contrasted sharply with the poverty and filth to be found on the outskirts of the city, which were dominated by an uncontrollable mass of shanty dwellings. The Habsburgs had always been more concerned with overseeing their over-stretched empire than in laying down any ordered plan for the adequate expansion of its capital, and money for development was increasingly short. The costliness of continual imperial campaigns and conflicts as Spain struggled against its gradual demise as a world power, along with a taxation policy from which nobles and the Church were exempt, resulted in soaring national debt. It would not be until the eventual conclusion of the Spanish Habsburg dynasty on the death of Charles II in 1700, and the arrival of the Bourbons in the figure of Philip V in 1714, that Madrid would experience any serious degree of economic and urban reform.

The grandson of Louis XIV of France, Philip V was unimpressed by Madrid in comparison to the grandeur of other European capitals. Its architecture was heavy and sombre, its streets dense and unsanitary, and the beleaguered Manzanares River could only be unfavourably compared with more magisterial examples such as the Seine. Municipal improvement was initially put in the hands of the Madrid governor, the Marqués de Vadillo, who with local architect Pedro de Ribera, embarked upon ambitious reform, including the building of the Puente de Toledo to ease access to the city. Raised at Versailles, however, and married to an Italian, Philip's tastes were inevitably the result of wider European influence, and when the Alcázar burned down in 1734, he swiftly commissioned the Palacio Real from Italian architects. The ultimate strategic transformation of Madrid into a city befitting its status as European capital was the work of his son, Charles III, previously King of Naples and a man of impassioned if despotic Enlightenment ideals. With the Italian architect Francesco Sabatini as his influential city engineer, Charles banned the dumping of waste in the open streets, and energetically set about a project of public improvements that included sewage collection, paving and street lighting. Such rudimentary sanitary reform would ultimately fail to keep pace with the continual growth of the urban population, but the neoclassical vistas and abundancy of monuments with which Charles also endowed the city have dominated its landscape ever since. In a triumph of Europeanism, the boulevards of the Paseo de Recoletos and Paseo del Prado, the Fountain of Cibeles, Sabatini's ceremonial gate the Puerta de Alcalá, and the scientific showcase of Spanish architect Juan de Villanueva's Museo del Prado (intended by Charles to be a natural history museum), became the architectural face of a majestic and prosperous Madrid, and indeed remain its most recognisable landmarks.

After Charles's reign the Bourbon monarchy fell into disarray, the result of the weakness of the new king, Charles IV, and the corruption of his chief minister Manuel Godoy. When Napoleon, sensing that Spain was thus ripe for expropriation, tricked the king and his ministers into a false alliance and invaded in 1808, the majority of state officials (along with Francophile intellectuals) thus offered little resistance. In a surge of patriotism, however, the Spanish population rose in indignant and passionate defence of its national autonomy, notably in the attack on the invading troops started by the local people of the traditional *barrio* of Maravillas in Madrid on 2 May 1808. Repressed by vengeful mass executions by the French the following day, the battle and the tragic events that followed were immortalised in the paintings of the same dates by Goya. Napoleon subsequently installed his brother Joseph Bonaparte as King of Spain, but as conflict continued and British forces joined the Spanish guerrillas, French rule was increasingly troubled.

Brief though it was, the French victory nevertheless extended European influence on Madrid. The immensely unpopular Bonaparte dedicated his short reign to rational urban improvements, and along with the important removal of burial grounds from the city centre, created numerous public squares, demolishing convents and monasteries in the process with an ardour that earned him the nickname of *El rey de plazuelas* [the King of Squares]. The return of the Bourbon monarchy in 1813, however, suspended any official attempts at the modernisation of either landscape or society, as the ideals of national independence quickly collapsed under the cruelly repressive regime of Ferdinand VII. The War of Independence had been a battle for freedom in which both popular traditionalism and radical liberalism joined forces in rejection of the French, and it brought forth a revolutionary Constitution, signed by an exiled national assembly in Cádiz in 1812. With the end of the conflict, however, conservative and liberal values parted company. Once returned to power, the apparently entirely contemptuous Ferdinand quickly reneged on the Constitution and became increasingly authoritarian, and with absolutist support rescinded many of the liberal reforms, hindering further political and social change. His reign left Madrid severely underdeveloped and, with the exception of Charles V's tree-lined boulevards, entirely archaic in appearance. What was perhaps his most significant urban commission, a cartographic model of Madrid completed in 1830, reveals a city of narrow, disorderly streets and shoddy buildings, against which the broad eastern avenues of the Paseo del Prado and Paseo de Recoletos stand in marked relief (Fig. 2).

If in Madrid urban development was at a standstill, elsewhere in Western society the social and physical landscape of the city was being significantly rewritten, the result of an emergent modernity and the newly authoritative vision of bourgeois society and liberal politics. Earlier paradigms and images no longer seemed

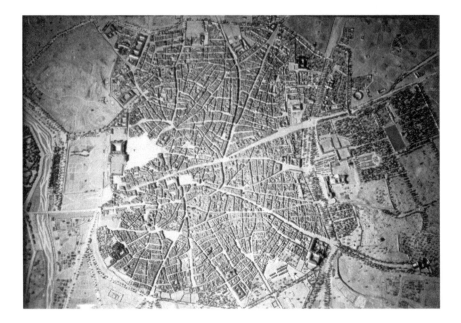

Figure 2 Model of Madrid (1831), Museo Municipal de Madrid

apposite to cities undergoing the effects of industrialisation and massive demographic explosion, and new modes of representation were sought that could provide form and meaning to the modernising, increasingly secular urban environment. A concern with writing and imaging the city, therefore, was coincident with urban change and manifest in an abundance of new genres. Whether volumes of practical, topographical information, historical chronicles, directories of streets and public buildings, illustrated manuals, or descriptions of social life and events, all assumed a familiarity with the city that promised to equip the reader with the knowledge necessary for traversing and understanding it. Such intelligibility would become increasingly contested as the century wore on, but in the first decades of the nineteenth century, with the escalating populations of major cities swelled by newcomers and foreign visitors, urban guides found a ready market. Priscilla Ferguson, for example, has described the importance of the genres of the *tableaux* and *physiologies* in reconceptualising the landscape of post-revolutionary Paris.[2] Presuming to elucidate the city for both eager visitors and bewildered local inhabitants alike, their narratives created the city as a text to be read, a representation that in turn would impact upon the living of its social and physical space. This chapter analyses two forms of urban representation that particularly characterised portrayal of Madrid during the first half of the nineteenth century: the urban plan or guide, and the journalistic vignette of everyday life, known in Spain as the *costumbre*.

Urban Guides

Early descriptive guides and tableaux of Madrid had appeared in the 1600s and remained consistently popular well into the nineteenth century. It was the publication of Ramón Mesonero Romanos' hugely popular *Manual de Madrid, descripción de la Villa y Corte* ('Madrid Manual, a Description of the Town and Court') in 1831, however, that initiated a new fascination with observing and cataloguing the city, boldly claiming to offer no less than a comprehensive, all-encompassing account of its past events and present landscape.[3] Previous writers, Mesonero states in his introduction, had failed in their attempts to write the history of Madrid:

> Some were excessively enthusiastic and partial to the fantastic, and did little more than create a tissue of fabulations, which, obscuring the light of reason, drew them into a labyrinth of errors. Others, less gullible and more rational, have tried to search for the truth and, lacking any certifiable facts, have rejected everything to do with those remote times.
>
> [Unos, demasiado entusiastas é inclinados á lo maravilloso, se complacieron en formar un tejido de fábulas, con las cuales, oscureciendo la luz de la razon, cayeron en un

laberinto de errors. Otros, menos crédulos y mas racionales, han procurado buscar la verdad, y á falta de datos conocidamente ciertos, han negado todo lo que corresponde á la época remota][4]

Mesonero's aim was to produce a companion to Madrid, informative about the city's myths and stereotypes, yet at the same time factual, functional and unprejudiced. As a study of the contemporary capital, he declared, it would not fictionalise the city, but neither would it be merely an inventory. As its title proclaimed, the *Manual* was to be a practical handbook for use in traversing the city, offering a summarised history and detailed topography. Moreover, for visitors, there was a list of hostels, cafés, shops, administrative institutions and cultural attractions, as well as a brief section on the character of the city and its inhabitants. Mesonero's claim that the *Manual* would be the supreme authority on Madrid, however, also manifested itself much more literally when, in an uncharacteristically conceited attempt to prevent plagiarism of his work, he seemingly petitioned for absolute narrative and intellectual rights to the city. The Consejo de Castilla rejected his demand that he be accorded exclusive authority as chronicler of its past, present and future as excessive and unreasonable, but the supremacy of Mesonero's influence was nevertheless already established. Stories and novels set in Madrid from the 1830s were typically dependent upon the exhaustive knowledge put forward in the *Manual*, which became almost as important for reference as the city itself. With the *Manual* Mesonero can be said to have 'invented' Madrid, with all the slippage between the material city and its representation that the term implies. For in mapping the social and spatial identity of Madrid, he in turn produced a conception of the city that would operate as both a future blueprint for architects and urban planners and a powerful narrative of traditional Madrilenian identity.

As the sub-title of the *Manual* indicates, Madrid was not a modern capital, retaining instead its pre-industrial identity as 'town and court'. The death of Ferdinand VII in 1833, however, and the regency of Maria Cristina, ushered in a new era, and a significant transformation of the laws, administration and habits of everyday life. With the new leniency, immigration began to soar after two decades of decline and Madrid suddenly found itself undergoing rapid demographic change. It quickly became apparent that the increaasingly cramped city, still contained within the limits of its sixteenth-century walls, was in urgent need of expansion and sanitary reform, as the cholera epidemic that swept through its streets in 1834 tragically illustrated. With the disentailment of church and crown land by liberal minister Juan Alvarez Mendizábal in the same year, over 1,000 properties in the city were quickly demolished, leaving a substantial area of land for rebuilding. Moreover, with the growth of a newly wealthy professional class of bankers, traders and other commercial speculators, fostered under Napoleonic rule and now strengthening into a pervasive social and political presence, there was a demand for a city landscape that reflected new commercial and secular interests. As large sectors of the city passed into the ownership of this emerging bourgeoisie, urban change on a large scale finally seemed feasible. In 1835 Mesonero thus published an appendix to the *Manual*, recommending numerous improvements along the lines of those he had seen elsewhere in Europe.[5] Madrid required expansion to the north and east, he declared, the building of wide avenues and squares, systematic street-naming and house-numbering, and the provision of pavements and street-lighting, as well as daily municipal cleaning. Moreover, if the city was to be the equal of the more elegant capitals of the rest of the continent, then it was crucial to create new commercial and leisure spaces, including shopping arcades and covered market buildings, public gardens, luxury hotels and theatres, as well as develop cultural facilities such as the popular press, libraries, literary and scientific institutions.[6]

Mesonero's urban vision was undoubtedly widely informed. In 1833 he had embarked upon a ten-month tour of major European cities, including Valencia, Barcelona, Gerona, Marseille, Lyon, Paris, London, Birmingham, Manchester and Liverpool, studying the science and aesthetics of contemporary urban planning. The seriousness with which his suggestions were met, however, was largely due to the swift and energetic support of the young mayor of Madrid from 1835 to 1836, Joaquín Vizcaíno, the Marqués de Pontejos. Official proponents of reform in the early nineteenth-century city unfortunately seem to have been doomed to only short periods of influence, and Pontejos was soon ousted by the political events of the late 1830s. Yet, by the time of leaving office, he nevertheless had initiated a significant programme of urban improvements. As Mesonero recalled in the 1844 edition of the *Manual*:

> New public buildings and monuments have been built, along with four covered markets, and the Fuente Castellana mausoleum; new squares and avenues have sprung up in the centre of the town and all the outlying areas; trees have been planted in the main streets and squares; and the cafés, shops and other public establishments show a taste and elegance previously unknown.
> [Se han construido nuevos edificios y monumentos públicos, cuatro mercados cubiertos, el mausoleo de la Fuente Castellana; se han formado nuevas plazas y paseos en el interior de la Villa y en todos los alrededores; se han plantado árboles en las calles y plazas principales; y en los cafés, las tiendas y demás establicimientos públicos se observa un gusto y elegancia desconocidos hasta entonces][7]

European visitors were less convinced by Madrid's sudden claims to sophisticated urbanity. Ford, for example, seems unimpressed by the radical liberalism and 'the disease of French polish' that he felt was obscuring the romance and colour of traditional Spain in the capital.[8] 'Madrid itself is but an unsocial, second-rate, inhospitable city', he complains, and 'when the traveller has seen the Museum, been to the play, and walked on the eternal roundabout Prado, the sooner he shakes the dust off his feet the better'.[9]

Théophile Gautier, visiting the city in 1840, is more positive, declaring the Prado 'one of the liveliest spectacles you can see . . . one of the finest boulevards in the world. Not for the site, which is quite ordinary . . . but for the surprising numbers of people who go there every evening'.[10] Gautier's emphasis is again, however, on the romantic aura of the city for the foreign traveller, for whom Spain was a quaint and primitive society, possessing a passion and spontaneity lost to 'civilized' modern Europe. If Madrid was experiencing political and material urban change, to the eyes of George Borrow, an Englishman who made several trips through Spain selling the New Testament on behalf of the British Bible Society in the late 1830s, its temperament and everyday life remained strikingly pre-modern. Dismissing the attempts to rationalise Madrid's urban landscape, for example, asserting that 'Petersburg has finer streets, Paris and Edinburgh more stately edifices, London far nobler squares', Borrow was far more struck by the exoticism of its people:

> But the population! Within a mud wall, scarcely one league and a half in circuit, are contained two hundred thousand human beings, certainly forming the most extraordinary vital mass to be found in the entire world; and be it remembered that this mass is strictly Spanish. . . . the huge population of Madrid, with the exception of a sprinkling of foreigners, chiefly French tailors, glove makers and peruquiers, is strictly Spanish, through a considerable portion are not natives of the place. . . . a population which, however strange and wild, and composed of various elements, is Spanish, and will remain so as long as the city itself shall exist. . . . Hail to you, valets from the mountains, mayordomos and secretaries from Biscay and Guipuscoa, toreros from Andalusia, riposteros from Galicia, shopkeepers from Catalonia! Hail to ye, Castilians, Extremenians, and Aragonese, of whatever calling! And lastly, genuine sons of the capital, rabble of Madrid, ye twenty thousand manolos, whose terrible knives, on the second morning of May, worked such grim havoc amongst the legions of Murat![11]

The passage is worth quoting at length, as it contains a valuable observation of the city's largely immigrant and traditional service population. For at the same time as Borrow ignores any claim to national autonomy on the part of Spain's different regions, proclaiming them all 'strictly Spanish', he nevertheless acknowledges the cultural multiplicity that is inherent to the identity of the capital. Again, of course, what he intends to celebrate is the exoticism of a lack of cosmopolitanism or universalising European influence, epitomised in the legendary resistance of the indigenous Madrid people against the might of Napoleon's troops. To liberal Spaniards, however, such orientalising descriptions were tiresomely ridiculous, and even if containing some truth were an image of Spain that exponents of modernization were keen to leave behind. On achieving an interview with Mend-izábal, then embroiled in civil war against the absolutist Carlists, who supported the claim of the pretender Don Carlos to the Spanish throne over the infant Isabel II, Borrow was told by the exasperated Prime Minister, who had little sympathy with religious conversion: 'My good sir, it is not Bibles we want, but rather guns and gunpowder, to put the rebels down with, and above all, money, that we may pay the troops'.[12]

Gautier, whose critical eye was both more discerning and more artistic than Borrow's, recognised in *castizo* Madrid not just a romantic ideal of national tradition, however, but also the trace of the past at the onset of modernity. Going in search of the famous Madrilenian *maja* or *manola*, the vivacious working-class beauty of Goya's eighteenth-century city, he finally finds her amongst the rag-pickers of the fleamarket, El Rastro:

> I looked for an authentic pure-blooded *manola* in all the corners of Madrid but I never found her. Once, as I was walking through the Rastro, and after passing many beggars who were sleeping on the ground in frightful rags, I found myself in a deserted alley, and there I saw, for the first and last time, the *manola* I was seeking. She was a handsome girl, about 24, the maximum age for a manola – like the *grisettes* or *modillistas* in Paris. She had a dark complexion, a glance that was steady and sad, slightly full lips and with something African about her features. Her long plait of hair was wound round her head and held with a comb. A cluster of coral hung from her ears. A necklace of the same material adorned her tawny neck. Framing her face and shoulders a mantilla of black velvet. . . . A red fan trembled like a scarlet butterfly in her fingers that were laden with silver rings. The last of the *manolas* turned the corner and disappeared from view, leaving me in wonderment at seeing in the real world a costume that could have come from the opera.[13]

To Gautier's modern *flâneur*, the last *manola* is not merely picturesque or exotic; rather she becomes an allegory of *castizo* Madrid, fascinating the nineteenth-century writer as she slips silently away from his gaze.

Sketches of Everyday Life

Despite European visitors' continued romanticism, urban changes in Madrid *were* encouraging a newly modern culture of public life and spectacle, based around a social landscape of cafés, theatres, squares and boulevards in which the new middle classes were prominently visible. Moreover, as elsewhere in Europe, the demand of this growing bourgeois population to look at itself was met by a proliferation of urban guides, historical studies and sketches of contemporary life. In contrast to the encyclopaedic handbook provided by the *Manual*, the journalistic genre of *costumbrismo* was characterised by brief and lively anecdotes of the social physiognomy of the city. With a national illiteracy rate of over 70 per cent even by the 1870s, the *costumbres* were aimed at the predominantly professional and educated readership of the new bourgeoisie.[14] Presenting the *castizo* culture of old Madrid alongside the social and political topography of a nascent middle-class city, they offered this urban public nostalgic scenes of a past to which they did not belong, and a literary reflection of the modern environment that they were themselves creating. Again the self-acclaimed leader of this new genre, itself a literary version of the urban guide, was Ramón Mesonero Romanos.

Mesonero's first collection of urban sketches, *Panorama Matritense* ('Madrid Panorama') (1835) collects together thirty-nine articles written in 1832 for the journals *Cartas Españolas* and *Revista Española*.[15] Of course such urban documentary-style fiction was not new to the nineteenth century. The figure of the professional city-dweller was a common device across Europe, in the hugely popular writings of Joseph Addison and Richard Steele in London, and of Étienne de Jouy in Paris, as Mesonero himself acknowledged.[16] Moreover, the humoristic representation of local life and customs already had a long tradition in Madrid, most famously in the work of the eighteenth-century playwright Ramón de la Cruz. What Mesonero was claiming by relating *costumbrismo* to a wider European tradition of urbane journalism, however, was the genre's modernity. As a fragmentary vignette of everyday urban life, written for a bourgeois readership and published in the popular press, the nineteenth-century *costumbre* was very much a modern and urban phenomenon. With the *Semanario Pintoresco Español*, the illustrated magazine launched by Mesonero in 1836 and under his direction until 1857, he defended the genre as both contemporary and aesthetically credible, publishing articles and reviews but predominantly *costumbres* from the most important and respected writers of the period. The *Semanario*, he announced, in contrast to a general tendency within the periodical press, was a primarily literary rather than political forum, 'exclusively *literary*, *popular* and *pictorial*, completely new to us in both essence and form' [exclusivamente *literaria*, *popular* y *pintoresca*, nueva absolutamente entre nosotros en la esencia y en su forma].[17]

The advertised apoliticism of the *Semanario* was undoubtedly in part an attempt to ensure a certain protection from censorship laws. Yet, along with Mesonero's insistent rejection of institutional politics throughout his life, it has led to the criticism of both writer and genre as conservative and traditionalist, and the term *costumbrismo* has generally come to imply a nationalistic nostalgia for a pre-industrial Spain. Many of its earliest examples, however, including those of Mesonero himself, were in fact concentrated on the present, concerned with depicting an urban society that was very much contemporary, and satirically critiquing its ineptitude in emulating the changes made across the rest of progressive Europe. That Mesonero conceived of the *costumbre* as a means of radical social comment is evident in the opening of his introductory article to the *Panorama*, where he states: 'It is a grave and delicate task, that of the author who sets out in his writings to attack the absurdities of the society in which he lives' [Grave y delicada es carga la de un escritor que se propone atacar en sus discursos los ridiculos de la sociedad en que vive] (*EM*, 3). Mesonero's writing style is ponderous and gains few favours from translation, but his sentiment is clear. For if most *costumbres* were little more than light dramatisations of stereotypical types and customs, propagating the mythic Spain evident in the travel accounts of foreign visitors such as Borrow or Gautier, for example, the best turned a discerning and critical eye to the values and morals of everyday Madrilenian life in the 1830s. Mesonero Romanos is himself undoubtedly accountable for the romantic image of traditional Spain, particularly in his later and more nostalgic *costumbres*. In his early pieces, however, both Mesonero and his contemporary Mariano José de Larra manipulated *costumbrismo* to write scathing satirical critiques of Madrid society and politics, and to express a proto-modern aesthetic of urban life. Their focus was the landscape of a city in transition, in which the traditions of old Madrid appear alongside new foreign influences, as part of a representation of the clash of customs, values, social relations and lifestyles. Through what was a predominantly picturesque genre, both writers attacked the inertia of their contemporary society and urged enlightened urban reform; Mesonero of a city he recognised as severely flawed in design and socio-economic structure, Larra of a society he regarded as culturally and politically provincial and tedious.

Panorama matritense begins with an attack on the stereotypical representations of a romanticised, quixotic Spain. Madrid as it is portrayed by foreign visitors for a foreign audience, Mesonero authoritatively complains, is completely unlike that known by the author of the *Manual*. The aim of his humble writings, he asserts, is to depict truthfully for the *Spanish* public, 'scenes of customs typical of our nation, and in particular of Madrid' [escenas de costumbres propias de nuestra nación, y más particularmente de Madrid](*EM*, 4). The title conformed to a fascination with panoptic spectacle in what Jonathon Crary has described as the increasingly optical consciousness of Western society in the eighteenth and nineteenth centuries, promising a similarly exhaustive profile of the city to that of the *Manual*.[18] One article from 1835, for example, 'Paseo por las Calles' ('A Walk through the Streets'), notes the common desire of the stranger to 'take in the full picture of the town on his first visit' [reconocer el aspecto general del pueblo que por primerea vez visita], and to find 'a central, elevated point, sufficiently high to allow them to survey and observe its layout from above' [conocer a un golpe de vista el conjunto del pueblo que los recibe, solicitasen subir a una altura céntrica y de la elevación correspondiente para medir y conocer avista de pájaro todo el plano de la capital] (*EM*, 304). There is only one place, he continues, that provides such a viewpoint in Madrid, the bell tower of the church of Santa Cruz, from which he (somewhat optimistically) suggests it would be possible to see as far as the Calle de Alcalá in the east, the Calle de Fuencarral to the north, the Calle de Mayor to the west, and the Calle de Toledo to the south, the streets that formed the approximate limits of the city before the expansion of 1860.

Observing Madrid from Santa Cruz, however, Mesonero then complains, gives only a general idea of the aspect of the city and its larger thoroughfares, one moreover that gives no sense of the inequalities and poverty of many of its dwellings. Interestingly, he does not suggest a simplistic opposition between the image of relatively regular urban form as seen from the panoramic perspective of the tower, and the chaos and confusion of the streets. For if the panorama gives an aspect of general beauty, it is a beauty that quickly becomes monotonous and uninteresting, and if the street is mean and plebeian, it is also heterogeneous and colourful. Descending to the streets, he recommends, allows the observer to see the variety of the city's built form, and the distinct dimensions and decoration of the facades of its houses. Moving from an encyclopaedic perspective to a kaleidoscopic one, from exhaustive description to the appreciation of colourful, changing form, the architectural example provides a synonym for Mesonero's writing of the social physiognomy of the city. For having provided his readers, in the *Manual*, with a map of Madrid, in the *costumbre* he declares, he intends to show them its character, to 'abandon stones for men; the conventions of architecture for the conventions of society; in short, the physical Madrid, for the essence of its people' [dejáramos las piedras por los hombres; los órdenes arquitectónicos por el orden de la sociedad; el Madrid físico, en fin, por el Madrid moral] (*EM*, 306).

Mesonero's sketches focus with fascination on the trivial aspects of everyday life. Under his fictional persona of El Curioso Parlante ('The Curious Chatterer'), he walks and writes the streets of Madrid incessantly, his footsteps, or those of his companions or interlocutors, being transformed into the words on his page. 'A prima noche' ('In the early evening'), for example, is a satirical account of contemporary idleness, a trait, Mesonero notes, for which the Spanish are famed, but that in the city is exacerbated by the temptation of numerous allures. Playing on the phrase 'to make time' [hacer tiempo] he depicts a Madrid full of time-wasters; the loiterers watching the clock in the Puerta del Sol, the dandy in front of the elegant shop in the Calle de la Montera, the bureaucrat smoking a cigarette and looking out of the window. El Curioso is interrupted while writing his article, however, by the arrival of don Pascual who, reading the piece, suggests that his friend is too harsh. Declaring that many activities generally regarded as a waste of time might have value if appreciated properly, he proceeds to give a long account of his own evening, which he has spent in various cafés and bars. However, other than the arousal of his senses by the smell of cigar smoke and coffee, the noise of political argument and the spectacle of dancing girls, he seems to have achieved very little. Pausing in his enthusiastic commentary, he notices that Señor Curioso is still writing – he has finished the article, copying down don Pascual's words and 'making time' from his friend's wasting of it. In Mesonero the city aroused not indolence but a zealous productivity. Yet the surrender to the city that the authoritative author himself continually resists or denies, constantly fascinates and provides inspiration.

Mariano José de Larra similarly attacked the phlegmatic stagnancy of Madrid society, often with a focus on the convoluted and backward economic and political structures that epitomised the provincialism of the city in the eyes of more cosmopolitan visitors. 'Vuelva usted mañana' ('Come back tomorrow') tells the plight of Monseiur Sans-Delai, a Frenchman who arrives in the capital for what he believes will be the swift completion of some administrative matters, leaving him time for sightseeing before his return home. Familiar with the phenomenal inefficiency of the city's bureaucracy, Fígaro knowingly laughs that he will be unlikely to accomplish his business within fifteen months. As the title of the piece implies, every errand in Madrid will take days to even initiate, as the harrassed Monsieur Sans-Delai soon discovers. Moreover, when his papers are then lost, Monsieur Sans-Delai, his name by now superbly ironic, is given a second piece of doom-laden advice: 'You can fill out a form' [Ponga usted un memorialito].[19] In a city that offers almost no services or facilities for outsiders, he is thus forced into idle waiting, left stranded by bureaucratic indolence and institutional incompetency. Mesonero's suggestions for urban reform dealt directly with the scarcity of adequate accommodation, restaurants and transport for visitors to 1830s Madrid, but the city's lack of official hospitality remained a common complaint. Richard Ford, for example, echoes Larra's satire of the Madrilenian official's lack of urgency when he recalls with frustration that, 'often when you have toiled through the heat and dust to some distant church, museum, library, or what not, after much ringing and waiting, you will be drily informed that it is shut, can't be seen, that it is the wrong day, that you must call again tomorrow.'[20] In contrast to Ford's pompous tourist, however, Larra is more self-reflexive in his condemnation. The piece ends with Fígaro's gloomy reflection on his own indulgence in the time-wasting that he has just so bitingly critiqued – the article 'Vuelva usted mañana' should have been delivered several months ago.

Larra's connection with *costumbrismo* has tended to be regarded with a degree of embarassment by literary critics, for whom it is little more than a popular yet inferior commercial genre.[21] The great yet tragic talent of Spanish Romanticism, who committed suicide at the age of twenty-eight as a result of a lovers' quarrel, his writing is very much a response to the specific conditions of 1830s Madrid, but it also manifests the recognisable social malaise of a broader European paradigm of urban modernity. The cosmopolitan tastes of the Francophile Larra are rarely stirred by the colour of Madrilenian low culture. Seldom fascinated by the picturesque, his satire is directed at the ridiculousness of Spanish society in comparison with an enlightened Europe, and is far more scathing than that of the humorous yet relatively indulgent Mesonero. To Larra's eyes, Madrid is a deformed approximation of European modernity, much as it still would be for Valle-Inclán decades later. Where Larra is at his most modern, and where he most parts company with Mesonero, is in his very conceptualisation of the 'everyday'. Unlike Mesonero, for example, for whom the present is the object of the observer's faithful rendition of contemporary life, for Larra the present by its very essence resists representation. If Mesonero seeks to explain and map the city, for Larra it is ultimately unexplainable and unmappable, because always present and thus ephemeral. It is this paradox that informs the latter writer's connection with an aesthetic of modernity typically associated with Baudelaire; the responsibility of the artist to capture what can only ever be fleeting and transient. Larra's aesthetic-isation of everyday life is just such a pose of modern urbanity, in which his writer-protagonist becomes a connoisseur of the ordinary and the banal. In the eyes of Francisco Umbral, for example, Larra is Madrid's *flâneur*: 'Larra has no home. We imagine him best in the street. The street is his home' [Larra no tiene hogar. Le imaginamos mejor en la calle. La calle es su hogar].[22] Mesonero by contrast is no *flâneur*, too jovial, too enamoured of Madrid's local colour and vibrancy to feel the alienation of a phantasmagoric modernity.

Neither is he simply a physiognomist, however. Mesonero's emphasis on objective social observation certainly anticipates the realist novel, and indeed would profoundly influence the work of the young Galdós. Yet, despite his notor-ious descriptive precision and ethnographic impulse, Mesonero was not oblivious to the *craft* of visual realism. As is often the case with generic categorisations, those writers generally regarded as most representative can also be those whose work is also the most idiosyncratic and self-questioning. Mesonero's writings are more than just examples of a comic picturesque, and alongside pieces of pure *costum-brismo* are hints that the city, sometimes, even for its supreme scholar, can be uncanny. In 'La Capa Vieja y El Baile de Candil' ('The Old Cape and the Dance of Candil'), for example, El Curioso visits the Rastro fleamarket with a companion, don Pascual Bailón Corredera, who suddenly recognises and purchases an old cape that he remembers owning as a young man. Don Pascual then tells Sr. Curioso of how during a period of youthful fascination with the dissipations of urban life, he would disguise himself as a *manolo* and, wearing the cape, explore the dissolute entertainments of the areas of Lavapiés and Barquillo: 'With it [the cape] I frequ-ented taverns and cheap restaurants, attics and brothels, lofts and rooftops, and without it I could have done none of these things. Such was the self-assurance this disguise gave me.' [Con ella frequenté tabernas y figones, buhardillas y burdles, palomares y azoteas, y sin ella nada de esto hubiera podido hacer: tal era la confianza que este *disfraz* me inspiraba.][23] El Curioso's self-righteous framing narrative condemns his friend's youthful indiscretion, but there is more than a little vicarious fascination in his writing of the tale. The memory of the power of the cape recovers for don Pascual a connection with the city that he has lost at the beginning of the story, and that finds resonance in Mesonero's explorations of the city of the present.

The notion of illusion occurs repeatedly throughout the *Panorama*. Several pieces, for example, focus on the social aspirations and pretensions of the middle classes and new bourgeois elite, Mesonero mocking their eager mimicry of high society, their desire for bureaucratic office jobs, and their ostentatious parade of luxury. Others continue the questioning of the reality of appearances through an engagement with illusion as aesthetic *form*. Public fascination with ocular attractions and entertainments was common across Europe in the early nineteenth century. Popular spectacles such as cosmoramas and polioramas had been introduced to Madrid in the 1700s, and *tutili-mundi* (show-booths) were a regular feature of the city's streets and plazas. Mesonero later recalled that the Diorama, erected in the Paseo del Prado in 1838, was one of the most popular and interesting attractions in Madrid, and a visual genre of 'admirable artistic production, the artifice of which is hidden absolutely from the spectator to create a complete illusion of reality' [admirable produccion artística, cuyo artificio se oculta absolutamente al espectador para constituirle en una completa ilusion de realidad] (*EM*, 395–6). The distinction of the real and the fantastic that Mesonero so regularly claimed to maintain in the *costumbre* collapses here, as indeed it often did in his own work.

One example of Mesonero's interest in the blurring of artifice and reality is the article 'Las Ferias' ('The Fairs'), which takes place during the period of the fiestas of San Mateo and San Miguel, yet manifests a far more self-reflexive treatment of the popular theme of the fair or fiesta than the picturesque *costumbres* common to both Mesonero and other writers. El Curioso is walking through Madrid with Señor Provinciano, a visitor to the city, who accuses him of only writing about the city in fair-time and never of ordinary daily life. They eventually arrive in the Plaza de Cebada, where they find a magic-lantern show surrounded by a fascinated crowd. 'And now you will see the main street of Alcalá at fair time' [Ahora van ustedes a ver la gran Calle de Alcalá en tiempo de ferias] (*EM*, 140), shouts the operator, beating a tambourine. Deciding that it would indeed be less exerting to look at the projection-picture of the calle de Alcalá than to walk across the whole city to see it in reality, they pay and look into the machine. The operator then begins his commentary, pointing out the size and grandeur of the avenue, its multitude of shops, stalls and people. To the bewildered eyes of his viewers, the magic lantern collapses the distinct spaces of the city, allowing the Calle de Alcalá in the west to apparently be seen from the Plaza de la Cebada in the south-east.

As the show finally comes to an end, the showman, who with supreme irony is blind, thanks his customers, 'the show is over, along with the fair' [esto se acabó, y la feria también] (*EM*, 140); whilst looking at the projected images of the fair in the machine, the real fair taking place in the city has passed. Madrid in fair-time is no more substantial than an image created by mirrors and described by a blind man, an artist of at once reality and illusion. If the diorama and the magic lantern were optical entertainments that attempted to create a perfect reproduction of everyday life, the contemporary *costumbre* similarly treated the city as a stage-set for brief scenes and tableaux that were carefully framed and choreographed. Benjamin, for example, describes the genre of the *feuilleton* as 'dioramic' liter-ature, 'individual sketches whose anecdotal form corresponded to the plastically arranged foreground of the dioramas, and whose documentary content corresp-onded to their painted background'.[24] The illusions of the fair reflect or are the same as those of everyday life, in which Mesonero himself, as *costumbrista*, is equally implicated: 'This world is a great fair, in which we all cast our lot' [Este mundo es una gran feria, en que todos traficamos] (*EM*, 135), El Curioso comments.

Ultimately, despite the implication of its title, *Panorama matritense* would seem to present a series of scenes of the city that question the legibility of the omniscient overview. There is only occasional focus on characteristic urban spaces (the Calle de Toledo, the Prado, the festival of San Isidro, the Puerta del Sol), almost none on specific 'types', and the perspective is typically that of the participant narrator El Curioso, rather than a detached and omniscient observer. Moreover, the city seems to *resist* overtly Mesonero's attempts at plain depiction and his constant pleas of objectivity. For the Madrid of *Panorama matritense* is not transparent. In both the depictions of traditional fiestas and entertainments, and the satires of modern interests and fashions, the city is a chimera. It appears to the author as a dream, a grand masquerade, a theatre of players, a series of images in a magic lantern show. Its inhabitants imitate, pretend, exaggerate, dissemble, wear masks. Even El Curioso Parlante wears a disguise. Despite his infinitely detailed descriptions of its materiality, Madrid remains elusive. The paradox of Mesonero's claim to represent the authentic and 'real' Madrid, is that the city itself is disingenuous.

Panoramic Visions

For Ramón Mesonero Romanos, writing *about* Madrid was also very much about *writing* Madrid. In 1846, as town councillor charged with the job of the reform and embellishment of the city, Mesonero began a new chapter in his chronicle of Madrid. His 'Proyecto de mejorales generales' ('Project of general improve-ments'), involved 'nothing less than a complete renovation of the capital within its former limits' [nada menos que una reforma completa de la capital dentro de sus límites de entonces].[25] Ambitious though his plans were, many were achieved within his lifetime, including reform of the Plaza Mayor, the clean-up of various slum areas, the creation of the Calle de Sevilla, which would become Madrid's financial centre, the building of a viaduct over the Calle de Segovia, and the conversion of the theatre of La Principe into the grand Teatro Español. He later stated in his autobiography, with somewhat rueful hindsight, that, 'I sincerely believe that I remained faithful, restricting my work to the proposal and support of those modifications I then deemed necessary, useful and above all feasible, and that I avoided getting carried away in an excess of enthusiasm' [creo sinceramente que me mantuve en el fiel, limitándome a proponer y sustentar aquellas modificaciones que entonces eran necesarias, útiles, y sobre todo practicables, sin dejarme arrastar de un entusiasmo delirante].[26] At the end of his three-year tenureship in December 1849, he left the town hall 'with the firm conviction of having done everything possible, to the best of the scant abilities of any good urban citizen, to promote the advancement and culture of the capital' [con la convicción de haber hecho todo lo posible, dentro de las escasas fuerzas de un buen ciudadano, en pro del progreso y cultura de la capital].[27]

If much of Mesonero's writing from this time, however, was dedicated to the constant suggestion of new projects and schemes for the betterment of the modern capital, an equal proportion was given over to remembering the eighteenth-century *Villa y Corte* whose rapid alteration he had himself initiated. *El Antiguo Madrid*, a series of articles published in the *Semanario* in the 1850s, and collected as a volume in 1861, presented 'historical-anecdoctal strolls through the streets and houses of this town' [paseos históricoanecdóticos por las calles y casas de esta villa].[28] Although gradually becoming a metropolis, Madrid was again being described as a 'town', as Mesonero anxiously recorded the streets, alleyways, dwellings, churches and palaces, fountains and monuments, gardens and markets, that were fast disappearing. During the extensive alteration of the Puerta del Sol between 1856 and 1862, for example, he reassures readers of its continuation as the city's emblematic centre:

> The Puerta del Sol is the very heart, the nucleus of the virility and action of court society. . . . the political, royal, scientific and literary laboratory of Madrid; . . . the stage on which the drama of its history and the intrigue of its intimate and social life are played out and reach their dénouement.
> [La Puerta del Sol es el corazón, el núcelo de la viralidad y animación de la población cortesana. . . . el laboratorio político, cortesana, científico y literario de Madrid; . . . la escena en la que se trazan y desenlazan las peripecias de su historia, las intrigas de su vida íntima y social].[29]

The Puerta del Sol was being transformed, almost unrecognisably, into the hub of the new commercial city. Mesonero, however, celebrates the square as not only the geographical focus of Madrid's contemporary social and cultural life, but also as the space in which the city's past is most available, traceable in the memories, stories and myths of its public history. A spatial symbol of the collective imagination of Madrid, a site that at once juxtaposed and provided continuity between the city's past, present, and future, the Puerta del Sol was indeed its 'degree zero', onto which all converged.

The paradox of the city map, as Iain Chambers describes, is that, 'with its implicit dependence upon the survey of a stable terrain, fixed references and measurement', it is inevitably undermined by the 'fluidity of modern life'.[30] Mesonero's attempt to record the old Madrid, to retain its traces within his own textual city, as well as his constant revisions and sequels to his other writings, suggest a frantic attempt to keep pace with the changing landscape of the city. He frequently drew attention to the corrections and changes he made in new editions, either by the sub-title of the latest volume or through the frame of a new introduction, reasserting his authority as Madrid's ultimate *cronista* in a market saturated with urban studies and guides. The *Manual de Madrid*, for example, became the *Manual histórico-topográfico, administrativo y artístico de Madrid* in 1844, appearing again in 1854 as the *Nuevo Manual* ('New Manual'). The volumes of *costumbres*, moreover, were also constantly annotated, *Escenas Matritenses* described in its third and fourth editions as 'corrected and augmented' [corregida y aumentada], and by its fifth edition in 1851 as 'the only complete edition, augmented and corrected by the author, and illustrated with fifty prints' [única completa, aumentada y corregida por el autor y ilustrada con cincuenta grabados].[31]

In contrast to the street-level perspective of the participant-narrator of the *costumbres*, Mesonero's plans and later histories of the city manifest a more detached and omniscient vision. From a focus on the city of the present, his writings turn to projects for its future and memories of its past. The reason for this is hinted in an essay, 'Adiós al lector' ('Goodbye to the reader'), originally published in 1862 as the prologue to a new volume, *Tipos, grupos y bocetos de cuadros de costumbres (Types, Groups and Sketches of Costumbres)*.[32] His earlier works, he admits, had been written by a younger man, and of a 'much simpler and quieter' [más sencilla y reposada] society. Now he finds that while his imagination has been enervated by age, society has continually 'rejuvenated and invigorated itself' [se ha rejuvenecido y vigorizado], changing 'each day in colour, countenance and manner' [cada día de colorido, de fisonomía, de intención].[33] With the constant reform and expansion of the middle decades of the nineteenth century, the authentic representation of a city that seemed to be ever-metamorphosing had become more difficult. Mesonero Romanos worked incessantly throughout his life towards the continued modernisation of Madrid. Yet as the years pass, the leisured, wandering observer of his *costumbres* seems less and less confident of his capacity to report the everyday life of the city – it is too varied, too constantly and dramatically changing – and returns instead to panoramic tales and recollections of the reliably *un*changing city of the past.

In desperation, Mesonero states, the *costumbrista* sought new modes of port-rayal: 'he looked to science for new ways of increasing the importance of his social studies and diversifying their form; . . . he searched his palette for richer colours' [pidió a la ciencia nuevos recursos para dar mayor importancia, forma diversa a sus estudios sociales; . . . buscó en su paleta colores más ricos]. Madrid, however, remained elusive:

> The tired painter pursues and studies it in vain, spying on its every move, its attitudes, its tendencies; his attempts are useless; society escapes from view; his model disint-egrates in his hands; impossible to catch it by surprise; only with recourse to the high-speed inventions of the age, steam power, photography and the electric spark, can he perhaps manage to keep pace with its rapid and meandering course; fix its ever-changing features on the canvas, establish instant mental communication.
> [En vano el pintor fatigado la persigue e estudia, espiando sus movimientos, sus actitudes, sus tendencias; trabajo inútil; la sociadad se le escapa de la vista; el modelo se le deshace entre las manos; imposible sorprenderle en un momento de reposo; y sólo echando mano de los progresos velocíferos de la época, del vapor, de la fotografía y de la chispa eléctrica, puede acaso alcanzar a seguir su senda rápida e indecisa; puede fijar sus volubles facciones en el lienzo; puede entablar con ella instantánea y mental comunicación].[34]

Finally, however, the beaten painter must admit defeat. 'Poor Madrid of my days! / Who can recognise you now?' [Pobre Madrid de mis días! / Quién te reconoce ya?], Mesonero wrote in a poem entitled 'El Nuevo Madrid' ('The New Madrid') in 1876, 'You have become sublime' [te has llegado a sublimar].[35] The pen [la pluma] that has both chronicled the mean Madrid of the past, and inspired the new Madrid of the present, however, is now 'rusty' [oxidada] and 'impotent' [impotente]. There were new media, he acknowledged, more suited to capturing the conditions of modernity, that now aspired to the panoramic vision that the anecdotal, 'dioramic' sketches of the *costumbre* could never achieve. As Benjamin comments, Daguerre announced the invention of the daguerrotype in 1839, the same year that his famous diorama in Paris burned to the ground.[36] Just as the diorama foreshadowed the photograph, the *costumbre* shaped, and then gave way to, the novel. In the articles that formed the chronicle of his own life, *Memorías de un setentón natural y vecino de Madrid* ('Memories of a seventy-year old native and inhabitant of Madrid'), Mesonero attempted to approximate the techniques of the camera. His articles became no longer observations of contemporary Madrid, fragments of life overseen or overheard by El Curioso Parlante as he participated within it, but 'photographic portraits' [retratos fotográficos] of the past city that Mesonero himself had known.[37] Serialised in the magazine *La Ilustración Española y Americana* between 1879 and Mesonero's death in 1882, *Memorias* formed not an autobiography as such, but rather memoirs of Madrid from his childhood until the end of his period of office as town councillor in 1850. There is no account of the period between this date and the time of writing: of the fall of the monarchy, the short-lived Republic or the Restoration. The city that Mesonero thus himself helped to form is ignored, and yet at the same time strangely present as the implicit environment from which he writes.

It is this juxtaposition of the traditional and the modern within the genre of *costumbrismo*, and above all the increasingly paradoxical relationship of the two in the work of Mesonero, that pervades the cultural production of the city as both a mythologised and lived space. The city, Maria Balshaw and Liam Kennedy importantly note, 'is inseparable from its representations', but at the same time 'is neither identical with nor reducible to them'.[38] The physical Madrid and its Romantic myth were indeed distinct, but in Mesonero's work they became inseparable, as he struggled between the twin impulses of his belief in Madrid's need for European reform and his nostalgia for its *castizo* past. Shifting between the roles of planner and author, his constant aim to create a lucid and functional map of the city, its history and its physiognomy, Mesonero initiated Madrid's awareness of itself, and was instrumental in forming its social, political and specifically urban consciousness. The late nineteenth-century Madrid, both *castizo* and bourgeois, that would be inherited by the eye and the pen of its new chronicler, Benito Perez Galdós, was truly to a large extent the literal as well as literary creation of Ramón Mesonero Romanos.

–3–

The Nineteenth-Century Capital

'How wonderful it would be to hold all the streets of Madrid in one glance' [Qué magnífico sería abarcar en un solo momento toda la perspectiva de las calles de Madrid], the young Benito Pérez Galdós wrote in the newspaper *La Nación* in 1865.[1] Echoing Mesonero Romanos, he recommends the bell-tower of Santa Cruz as the site for such a panorama, although again his tone is arch, recognising the superficiality of the bird's-eye view even while he aspires to its promise of totality. For Galdós, the writer of the city required more than a panorama or blueprint; he needed a telescopic vision that could penetrate into the depths of streets and buildings. Like Mesonero, Galdós would also descend from the heights of Santa Cruz to the street, and he too would pose as a dramatised narrator of contemporary Madrid. Whereas the older writer channelled the conflicting interests of everyday urban life and modern urban planning into separate discourses, however, Galdós represented the clash of the *castizo* and the bourgeois within the narrative of the modernising city. Another interminable walker, Galdós revelled in abandoning himself to the street, yet he also desired the panoptic omniscience promised by the tower of Santa Cruz: 'to see who enters and leaves, who prowls, watches and lies in wait' [ver el que entra, el que sale, el que ronda, el que aguarda, el que acecha]. Within the part-material and part-imaginary Madrid of the novel, he attempted to reconcile the two.

In the era of the *costumbre*, Galdós states in his novel *Fortunata y Jacinta* (1886), 'For all its ridiculous vanity, Madrid was a metropolis in name only' (*FJ*, 28), masquerading as a European capital. '[A] bumpkin in a gentleman's coat buttoned over a torn, dirty shirt', it was yet 'about to become a real gentleman' (*FJ*, 28). The city that Galdós observed from the tower of Santa Cruz in 1865 was no longer that of 1828, but instead a new secular landscape rising from the land cleared by disentailment and on the point of expansion. The inauguration of the first railway line between Madrid and Aranjuez in 1851 had initiated industrial and economic growth, and the beginning of work on the Canal de Isabel II in the same year assured a regular water supply that the beleaguered Manzanares river could not provide. Constitutional and bourgeois Madrid, however, required an urban scenography that would symbolise its developing modernity. The Puerta del Sol was remodelled into the commercial, administrative and financial heart of the city, and new public squares were created, including the plazas of Santa Ana, Pontejos, del Rey and de Los Mostenses. To the south, the arrival of the rail industry resulted in a belt of factories and workshops between the early stations of Atocha, del Norte and Delicias, and to the east, the elegant Paseo de Recoletos extended into the wide, north–south boulevard of the Castellana. The liberal and mercantile ideologies of the new city were perhaps best represented, however, by two buildings, both designed by the architect Pascual y Colomer; the city's parliament, the Palacio del Congreso, erected on the Calle de San Jeronimo in 1842, and the extensive residence built for the Marqués de Salamanca on the Paseo de Recoletos between 1846 and 1855. A wealthy banker and entrepreneur, the Marqués de Salamanca was the embodiment of Madrid's new commercial elite and a principal instigator of progress. It was his financial backing that promoted the Madrid–Aranjuez railway line in 1851, and the initial expansion of the city in the 1860s. The Palacio de Congreso and the Palacio de de la Marqués de Salamanca epitomised the principles of democracy and private enterprise. Built to the east of the city, in symbolic counterpart to the royal palace in the west, they formed an architectural overture to the era of modernity.

'Everything nowadays is new,' Galdós wrote of Madrid in 1870, five years after the piece in *La Nación*, 'and the society Mesonero described today seems almost as remote as the fables of antiquity'.[2] The types and traditions of the *costumbres* no longer resonate for Madrid in the 1870s, he argues, and 'the new elements which political reforms have introduced into society, the rapid disclosure of certain ideas to even the lowest classes, the ease with which a passive and vividly imaginative populace like ours assimilates certain customs, all make the task of portraying them harder and more complicated'. The customs of contemporary society are instead those of a culturally hegemonic, urban middle class, which it is the task of the novel, he asserts, to portray:

> it is the middle-class, so neglected by our novelists, which is our model, our inex-haustible source. The social order nowadays is built on the middle-class: through its initiative and intelligence it has taken on the sovereign role in all nations; it is there that nineteenth century man is to be found, with all his virtues and vices, his noble, insatiable aspirations, his passion for reforms, his frantic activity.[3]

The pervasiveness of this middle-class culture, however, made for a multilevelled and complex bourgeois society, that extended from the beggary of those down on their luck, to the aspirations of the petit bourgeoisie, the pretensions of a middle group constantly mortgaging itself to an appearance of leisured superiority, and the affluent business elite gradually integrating through marriage with an aristocracy in decline. The distinction between these levels is one of money and status, or at least the appearance of money and status. For of all Galdós's criticisms of Madrid society – its false values, intolerant and conservative Catholicism and poor quality of education – the most relentless is his condemnation of its common pretence to a material status and power it does not possess.

The conception of the new Madrid by the liberal order was that of a planned and rational space, with an infrastructure that facilitated the circulation of both people and goods. The arrival of the railway heralded a new era of modernisation, and by 1865 the city's rail network extended throughout Spain and into France, encouraging economic and urban growth. The new spatiality of the city symbolised, but also generated, new configurations of sociality and subjectivity. The tree-lined *paseos* and gardens, for example, originating from the health-conscious ideals of urban planners yet used by an aspiring elite as spaces for social display, provided the bourgeoisie with the means to consolidate their status and identity through a visual culture of seeing and being seen. Market-places, taverns and street fairs, the traditional public social spaces of the populace, were joined by the cafés, shopping arcades, theatres, exhibition halls and railway stations that were beginning to characterise the metropolitan geography of a modern Madrid, fashioning a new culture of middle-class urbanity.

The escalating population, however, continued to present a significant social problem, as despite the changes prompted by disentailment, the city remained suffocated within the delimited area of its 1625 walls. Recognising the need for further extensive reform, the town council thus instructed chief city engineer Carlos María de Castro to draw up a proposal for the future expansion of the city and its infrastructure. Castro's 1860 plan for the *Ensanche de Madrid* ('Madrid Extension') proposed enlargement to the north, north-east and south, increasing the city's size threefold. In addition it recommended the extension and widening of the Paseo de la Castellana into a north–south arterial boulevard that, with the Calle de Alcalá, would facilitate access and circulation between the *Ensanche* and the centre of the city.[4] The new areas were organised according to use and function, with residential districts for the rich and middle classes in the north, and industrial and agricultural zones in the south. Enthusiasm for the project was mixed. Despite Castro's genuine intention to create a hygienic and orderly city, in which living conditions were considerably improved across social groups, his plan proposed a socially segregated urban map that offered little change to the chaotic conditions of the city centre. The cost of the project was high, and few financial backers (with the notable exception of the Marqués de Salamanca) were prepared to risk investing in such a venture. Madrid's aristocracy and new bourgeois elite, moreover, showed little inclination towards moving out of the cramped yet lively Madrid *vieja* ('old Madrid') of the city centre for Castro's orderly yet subdued suburbs. The plan was as a result only ever partially realised, and many of its environmental ideals (such as the restriction of building heights and the provision of gardens and courtyards) were drastically cut. Some areas did begin to develop fairly quickly, however, such as the middle-class districts of Chamberí and Argüelles, and the elegant bourgeois residential district to the east of the city named after Salamanca, whom it finally bankrupted. Castro's *Ensanche* translated the growing social and economic dominance of Madrid's bourgeois elite into the stone of the urban map, at the same time as it became a memorial to their ruin.

The 1880s mark a distinct epoch in Galdós's writing, influenced by his voracious reading of Zola and the deterministic modern urban mythology of literary naturalism. Having written two series of highly successful and relatively patriotic historical novels, the *Episodios Nacionales* (*National Episodes*), with *La desheredada* (*The Disinherited*, 1881) he began a new focus, known as the *novelas contemporaneas* (contemporary novels), a critique of the social, political and spatial history of bourgeois Madrid from the fall of Isabel II in 1868, through the short constitutional monarchy of King Amadeo and the even briefer period of the Republic, to the Restoration of the Bourbon monarchy in 1875. Surveying this turbulent period from the relative economic and social stability, yet political corruption, of the authoritarian 1880s, the contemporary novels depict the city as the site and text of fantasy, folly and disillusionment. Far more overt in depicting the poverty, sordidness and immorality of Madrilenian life than his earlier writing, Galdós's new style drew accusations of unmitigated naturalism and obscenity from reactionary quarters. Describing the influence of Zola on *La de Bringas* (*That Bringas Woman*, 1884), for example, one reviewer complained:

> Details overwhelm the whole; design, plot, and dramatic interest have given way to analysis, description and inventory; form drowns out content; the whore has supplanted the lady, the rabble has replaced urbane society, and vices have taken the place of passions.[5]

For more radical critics this was not a bad thing, the novelist and critic Leopoldo Alas (Clarín), enthusing that,

> It is the first time that one of our good novelists has dealt with this poverty-stricken, fetid Madrid, prey to hunger and humiliation, which on the one hand is close to the barbaric and all its aberrations, and on the other seems to express the pestilential decadence of an exhausted race that once possessed a refined culture. In *La desheredada* this Madrid is sometimes portrayed as a throwback to some African race, full of terrible passions, but is also shown to be the rubbish tip that is the necessary part of our modern capitals.[6]

Galdós's Madrid is, for Alas, a degenerate space, epitomising the atavism of modern civilisation, in which there seems little to choose between the barbarism of the primitive, and the waste and refuse that is the nadir of bourgeois modernity.

Yet, if the contemporary novels are Zolaesque in their material descriptiveness, their social-scientific focus on the influence of heredity and environment, and their relation of personal histories to the broader social and political climate of city and nation, they also stress a fantasy and illusion in the experience of everyday life that updates the quixotic tradition of Spanish literature for the contemporary city of modernity. Fiction and reality continually blur in Galdós's representation of Madrid, as he writes of a city that he found as illusory in real life as in the pages of the novel. In an early manuscript for *Fortunata y Jacinta*, he described the biography of the Santa Cruz family that opens the novel and serves as a microsocm of the history of bourgeois Madrid, as a 'replica of the reality that I am creating' [simulacro de la realidad que estoy haciendo].[7] The use of the word 'simulacro', however, hints at the frequent self-reflexivity that makes Galdós's realism so fascinating and paradoxical. For Galdós the craft of fictional realism paralleled the illusory nature of Madrid life itself, and his writing constantly questions any transparent representation of this urban society even as it represents and affirms it. The Madrid of *Fortunata y Jacinta* is thus not only a 'realistic' model in miniature of the social, political and economic history of the city. It also reflects the fictionality that Galdós recognised to be part of the actuality of the city itself. The city of disentailment and the *Ensanche* was indeed a 'capital of the nineteenth century', a phantasmagoria of liberal capitalism, socioeconomic exchange and reification, protected by the disciplinary control of deviant social types and bodies. The Madrid that Galdós creates in his novels, as he was well aware, is a facsimile of a city that was itself a chimera.

Bourgeois Madrid

City space is omnipresent in Galdós's novels, most obviously as a common structural and plot device, interlinking both novels and distinct class and social areas through the relationships and trajectories of the characters who move between them, yet also as a marker of financial status, cultural taste and changing fortune, all the more important in a society that he repeatedly portrays as an endless masquerade. More broadly, however, it is the variety and complexity of communication, encounter and flow across the city (and beyond), that identifies the city as a socio-spatial formation, the product of the interaction of built form, social rhythms and human practices and emotions. The city and its inhabitants, Galdós recognises, are mutually constitutive. The successful rise of the Santa Cruzs, for example, from ownership of a modest fabric shop at the end of the eighteenth century, to leading members of Madrid's mercantile business aristocracy by the middle of the nineteenth, coincides with disentailment, the growing financial power of the middle-class, and the creation of the social and physical landscape of a secular city of modernity:

> it was the era when the middle class was beginning to come into its own, taking up the
> jobs created by the new political and administrative system, buying up all the properties

(of which the Church had held the title) with instalment plans, thus making itself the chief landowner and beneficiary of the budget; in a word, gathering the spoils of absolutism and clericalism to found the empire of the frock coat. (*FJ*, 28)

Madrid's textile business provides a metaphor for this transition from tradition to modernity, as domestic fabrics are superseded by foreign imports, oil lamps in the offices and warehouses by gas lighting, hard currency by bank notes and credit, Asiatic craftsmanship and trade by cheap mass markets, and the Madrileña's vividly coloured manila shawl by the bourgeois European gentleman's sober frock coat. The cloth trade remains a marker of change throughout the novel, moreover, as with the onset of the Restoration and consequent increase in bourgeois confidence, fashions become more elegant and flamboyant, 'finery appearing in the streets of Madrid and in political circles due to the change of government' (*FJ*, 510).

Madrid's commercial elite was on the whole, however, much less energetic than the Marqués de Salamanca in establishing a distinct identity and place for itself. In Galdós's contemporary histories the *Ensanche* grows silently on the periphery of both city and events, as the Madrilenian aristocratic and business elites continue to live side by side with the city's lower-classes in the old city centre. The Santa Cruzs, for example, live in the Plaza de Pontejos, in close proximity to the Plaza Mayor and calle de Toledo where they mix with the people of the *pueblo*. A 'rich and terribly respectable family', they yet have friends 'in all spheres, from the highest to the lowest', revealing the social indeterminacy of a society in which 'aided by bureaucracy, poverty, and education, all classes have gradually mixed' (*FJ*, 81), the infinite, indefinite strata of the bourgeoisie coalesce imperceptibly, as 'threads cross, get lost, and reappear where you'd least expect them' (*FJ*, 81). The bustle of this multifarious urban life was seemingly more appealing than Castro's ordered, spacious suburbs and Salamanca's modern sanitation systems, for it was over a decade before the middle-classes overcame their reluctance to move out of the cramped city centre. Barbarita Santa Cruz, for example,

> [would not] have exchanged 'that corner of Madrid' where she had been born, for any of the flamboyant sections of town that enjoyed the reputation of being airier and cheerier. No matter what they said, the Salamanca neighbourhood was *country*. The good lady was so fond of the suburb that was her native land that in her mind she wasn't really living in Madrid unless she could hear . . . the uproar of mail coaches every morning and afternoon, the constant echo of the hubbub on Postas Street. (*FJ*, 85)

Her preference for the noise of the city over the comfort and calm of the outlying district of Salamanca replicates that of Rosalía de Bringas in *Tormento*, who similarly asserts:

No one will drag me away from this district. Nothing outside this little corner seems to me like Madrid. I was born in the Plaza de Navalón and for a long time we lived in the Calle de Silva. When two days go by without my seeing the Plaza del Oriente, Santo Domingo el Real, the Incarnation and the Senate, I don't seem to have been alive. I don't think I get any benefit from the Mass unless I hear it in Santa Catalina de los Donados or the Chapel Royal or the Buena Dicha. I admit this part of the Costanilla de los Angeles *is* rather narrow but I like it like that. We seem to have more company when we can see our opposite neighbours so close that we could almost shake hands. I like to have neighbours on all sides. I like to hear the tenant running up his stairs at night; I like to hear people breathing above me and below me. I find solitude quite terrifiying and, when I hear about families who have gone to live in that suburb of Sacramental that Salamanca is laying out beyond the Plaza de Toros, it gives me the shivers. Goodness how frightening. Now this place is like a public balcony. Such a bustle![8]

One of the more regularly surfacing characters in Galdós's novels, Rosalía is admittedly an insufferable snob, whose preference for the area around the royal palace manifests her pretensions to the traditional aristocracy. This passage, however, not only expresses her class condescension towards the 'new-monied' *barrio* of Salamanca, but, also an affectual, everyday relationship with the old centre of the city that contrasts with the antipathy with which it was regarded by enlightened urban planning. For both Rosalía and Barbarita, the apartment blocks of Madrid *viejo* possess a sociability that the private mansions of the suburbs denied. The streets, walls and balconies of the city centre, seemingly breathing with people, embody for both women the very 'citiness' of Madrid.

The affective relationship with the city demonstrated by Rosalía de Bringas and Barbarita Santa Cruz is common among Galdós's female characters, who spend a considerable amount of their daily time in energetically traversing the city, on their way to attend mass, visit friends or charitable institutions, or to shop in the markets, stores and boutiques clustered around Sol and the Plaza Mayor. The various journeys of these women create busy networks of social and economic communication across Madrid. In *Fortunata y Jacinta*, for example, the charitable work of Guillermina Placheco, who lives next door to the Santa Cruz family in Pontejos, provides a consistent link between the wealthy elite of the city centre and the poor areas of the Plaza Mayor and Calle de Toledo. Guillermina also connects the Santa Cruz family with the women's reform convent, the Micaelas, where the lower-class Fortunata resides before her marriage to Maxi Rubín, and where she first sees Jacinta, her lover Juanito Santa Cruz's wife. Guillermina's urban network extends as far north as the recently developed suburb of Chamberí, where she passes the balcony of the Rubín household on her way to the orphanage on the Calle de Albuquerque, Doña Lupe Rubín having moved from the more expensive Salamanca (where she must have been an early resident) in the early 1870s.

Towards the end of the novel, when Doña Lupe moves again, this time to the more central Lavapiés, in the south of the city, she is surprised to see the familiar figure of Guillermina passing her window here too, on her way to the tenements of the Puerta de Toledo. The plots of the novels are largely driven by chance meetings that occur within these networks of places and streets, as characters cross paths between their different destinations. The transitivity of the city as a space of local, domestic interaction for these women, contrasts sharply with the gridded streets of the new bourgeois city symbolised by the male figures of Castro and Salamanca.

The multiple connections of urban spaces and networks, which Galdós asserts above all by his practice of using a large yet common cast of characters across the contemporary novels, are not only registered and manifest through walking or wandering. Galdós also has a keen ear for the aural map of the city. Doña Barbarita, for example, learns of Juanito's affair with Fortunata from his sudden use of the crude language of the milieu of urban low-life. It is perhaps economic exchange, however, that is the most dominant mode of communication in the modern city, and in which again Galdós presents women rather than men as the more active; not only as shoppers in Madrid's markets or boutiques, but also as participants within a system of financial transactions conducted through the more indirect means of letters, messengers and go-betweens. In *La de Bringas*, for example, Rosalía is forced to engage with pawnbrokers and the sly usurer Torquemeda as a result of her reckless practice of buying on credit, while in *Fortunata y Jacinta* Doña Lupe is a secret money-lender herself, enjoying a lucrative business through the intermediary of the same Torquemeda.

Men, in contrast to the women of Galdós's novels, are rarely depicted wandering the city streets or engaged in direct financial transactions, and indeed seem to have very little active presence within the city in general. The masculine space of Galdós's Madrid is the café, which functions as a nodal point for male characters both within and across the novels. The café and its *tertulia* was a ubiquitous and distinctive feature of the cultural, social and political life of Madrid throughout the nineteenth century. There were over eighty establishments in the city in 1881, the highest concentration in and around the Puerta del Sol, leading one guide to comment that 'Few towns have quite as many cafés as Madrid' [Pocas poblaciones tendrán un número de cafés tan considerable como Madrid].[9] Places for reunion and discussion more than actually eating or imbibing, many retained a regular clientele that endowed each with a particular atmosphere or inclination. Of some of the earliest, the Fontana de Oro was known for its fierce political debates, the Príncipe for its intellectual circle, and the Levante as the haunt of chess and draught-players.[10] Galdós devotes an entire chapter of *Fortunata y Jacinta* to an extended depiction of the camaraderie and indolence of the café, and the tertulia's celebration of talk for its own sake:

Gross banalities as well as ingenious, discreet, and pertinent ideas may be heard in these places, for they are frequented not only by rakes and swearers; enlightened people with good habits go to cafés too. . . . In a café one hears the stupidest and also the most sublime things. . . . It's not all frivolity, stale anecdotes, and lies. The café is like a grand fair where countless products of the human mind are bought and sold. Naturally there are more trinkets than anything else; but in their midst, and sometimes going unnoticed, there are priceless gems (*FJ*, 439).

The café here becomes the collective brain of the city, into which knowledge is poured and consumed. Ultimately however, it merely mirrors the commercial street, true intellect mixing with a sham erudition gained from the appropriation and assimilation of the ideas of others, and all spaces and relationships within the city equally pervaded by the exchange values of modern society.

By the middle of the nineteenth century most cafés were commodious, ornately decorated and lit with numerous gas lamps. Juan Pablo Rubín spends most of every day at the café, and '[t]he nook and its atmosphere had become so vital to him that only when he was there did he feel in full possession of his faculties'(*FJ*, 433). An almost exclusively male domain, for Rubín it offers a surrogate domesticity, epitomising the semi-public interior that Benjamin would characterise as the domicile of the nineteenth-century *flâneur*:

The café gave him a feeling of privacy that usually comes from one's own home. When he entered all the objects smiled as if they belonged to him. He fancied that the people he saw there constantly – the waiters, the headwaiter, certain regular customers – were closely related to him by family ties. (*FJ*, 433)

When the favoured café of the moment changes, either due to a quarrel, to unreasonable demands by a waiter for payment, or to 'certain inexplicable emigration currents common in the society of lazy men', 'it was like moving to a new house . . . Juan Pablo took his domesticity wherever he went, and after patronizing a new café for a few days he felt at home there' (*FJ*, 433). During a period of five years he frequents at least eight establishments, most near the Puerta del Sol.

With implicit reference to the criticisms of Mesonero, Galdós makes plenty of deprecatory remarks about the café environment. He describes Rubín as 'an implacable, persistent assassin of time; his only deep joy consist[ing] of watching the hours die gaspingly' (*FJ*, 433). The political discussion and gossip of Rubín's *tertulia* is little more than a pretext for lazy sociability, a reflection of the empty rhetoric that has become part of Restoration governmental politics itself. Referring to the 'tacit agreement' to alternate power made between the Conservative and Liberal politicians Antonio Cánovas del Castillo and Práxedes Mateo Sagasta, for example, the narrator remarks that 'political morality is like a cape with so many patches that one no longer knows which was the original fabric' (*FJ*, 435). In the political as much as in the commercial sphere, nothing is what it seems. 'It's all a farce', the sceptical Feijóo comments, 'and it's only a matter of knowing who gets perks and who doesn't' (*FJ*, 435).

The café is thus less a space of flow and encounter in the city, than of stasis and familiarity, the meetings and discussions that take place there never furthering either dramatic or political events as they promise. In what is almost a throw-away line in *Fortunata y Jacinta*, the reader is informed that among the habitués of the Café Suizo is the idle Juanito Santa Cruz, who along with Joaquín Pez and Sánchez Botín, both lovers of Isidora Rufete in *La desheredada*, 'had started the wittiest, liveliest *tertulia* that had ever existed in the cafés of Madrid' (*FJ*, 515). Despite the obvious existence of a male fraternity within the city's café network, however, this plays almost no part in the plots of the novels, other than in the securing of civil administrative posts. Yet the café appears constantly in the background of the *novelas contemporaneas*, a reminder of the dominance of a male infrastructure of aristocratic, professional and bureaucratic authority: 'Wherever there are men there is authority, and these café authorities, who sometimes define, sometimes predict, and always influence the crowd because their opinions are apparently sound, constitute a sort of consensus' (*FJ*, 436). In a turbulent political climate in which beliefs are unstable and allegiances are inconstant, the café and the *tertulia* yet remain established centres of the pervasive power of a masculine bourgeois order.

The Street and the Madrileña

Galdós's contemporary novels regularly testify to the existence of an incipient yet vibrant Madrilenian consumer culture, in which shopping was a seductive and addictive activity. Indeed, although Zola's *Au Bonheur des Dames* (1883) offers the ultimate dramatisation of material desire as the irresistible seducer of women through the vast, spectacular space of the department store, *La desheredada*, written two years before, already presents shopping as an activity in which women were seen to indulge with sensual and irrational pleasure. Urban and economic growth across Europe was resulting in a new industry of consumerism, and women quickly became the objects of a visual culture of consumer marketing. Depictions of women in the nineteenth-century Spanish press were characterised, as Lou Charnon-Deutsch has shown in her study of the illustrated Spanish press in the nineteenth century, by a 'surfeit of images depicting elegant, exotic, idle, and alluring women', through which 'working-class women were rendered invisible, while women of the leisure classes were incited to self-spectacle and extravagant consumption'.[11] The retail spaces that Galdós describes, however, are significantly different from the department stores that have become ubiquitous in narratives of the history of European consumption in the late nineteenth century. The narrator of *Fortunata y Jacinta*, for example, complains of the city's 'lack of "big stores"' (*FJ*, 633). Of course not all retail outlets, even within Paris, followed the sales principles or equalled the multi-department interior phantasmagorias of the Bon Marché, and the ultimate principles of selling in the department store, based on theatrical and seductive display, the lure of bargain prices for luxury goods, and the creation of a public space of sociability, were common amongst retailers in European capitals, if not practised all at once and on the same vast scale.[12] Accounts of commercial Madrid from the late nineteenth century indicate a distinct shopping culture in which independent shopkeepers and family businesses, market stalls and intinerant traders remained prominent.

At the beginning of chapter 7 of *La desheradada*, Isidora Rufete takes a long walk through the commercial heart of Madrid. The pretext for her sojourn is to attend mass at the Iglesia de San Luis, although in reality, 'she had come out for the sake of it, in order to see noisy, bustling Madrid, the mirror of so much happiness, its streets filled with light, its endless shops, its people with nothing to do who come and go in a perpetual leisurely stroll' (*D*, 109). For Isidora, the city is a commercial pleasure zone in which she can wander and consume with freedom and delight. Along the calles de Hortaleza and Montera, 'looking into shop windows, attracted by anything pretty, rich or sumptuous', she revels in their infinite bazaar of opulent commodities:

> rich furs, endless fine clothes, ties, trinkets that enchant the eye with their strangeness, objects that combine invention and patient industry, putting to use gold, silver, nickel, Russian leather, celluloid, cornelian, jet, amber, brass, rubber, coral, steel, satin, glass, talc, mother-of-pearl, shagreen, porcelain and even horn . . . exotic furniture inlaid with ivory, oak carves in feudal style, inlaid walnut, majestic double beds and finally, bronzes, ceramics, clocks, cruets, candelabra. (*D*, 111)

Entitled 'Taking possession of Madrid', the chapter depicts Isidora's limitless material desires, but also the irony of her aspirations to this city of material wealth and comfortable leisure. Far from a wealthy consumer, Isidora is in fact a provincial parvenu from La Mancha, who believes herself to be the illegitimate daughter of a noblewoman and who has arrived in the city to demand recognition and inheritance. Like Flaubert's Emma Bovary she is a voracious reader of the romantic serial novel, and an uncritical acceptance of its rags-to-riches tales of beautiful young women has convinced her of the inevitable success of her claim. Internalising the image of the high-society woman as fashionable and leisured consumer to be found in the popular press, her vanity and self-importance incline her towards material and sensual pleasure. The goods on display in the shop windows, described as 'gaudy superfluous rubbish' (*D*, 111) by the narrator, glitter enticingly before Isidora's fantasising eyes, the reflection of her body in the glass seemingly adorned with the goods on display. In her vanity and self-absorption she creates herself in terms of objects, engaging in an act of self-commodification for her own consumer fantasies. As Rachel Bowlby notes in her study of consumer culture in the naturalist novel, '[t]hrough the glass, the woman sees what she wants and what she wants to be'.[13] Isidora's devouring gaze quickly turns into overwhelming desire, '[s]he had to buy something, a little something', the purchase of a parasol rapidly followed by gloves, a fan, a brooch, earrings, a purse, perfume, hair-pins, a comb and embossed note-paper, as the limits of her pocket are overcome by an insatiable appetite for extravagant commodities.

If Isidora buys voraciously and with uncontrolled abandon, many of Galdós's other female protagonists embody different stereotypes of consumerism. For Barbarita Santa Cruz in *Fortunata y Jacinta*, for example, shopping is a favourite pastime raised to the level of an art form:

> Barbarita's craze was buying. She cultivated art for art's sake, or in other words, buying for buying's sake. There was nothing she liked better than going on a shopping spree and coming home laden with purchases that, though not exactly superfluous, weren't absolutely necessary either. (*FJ*, 92)

Unlike Isidora's reckless spending, however, Barbarita's 'vice' never extends beyond her purchasing power, considerable though that is. Always watchful for a 'good deal' (*FJ*, 95), her purchases are informed and business-like, carefully researched by Estupiñá, and, as the narrator states, 'her masterful art of being a rich customer stemmed precisely from this control' (*FJ*, 92). Barbarita, far from becoming a passive victim of the manipulations of consumer society, critically negotiates the practices of selling and buying, her pleasure stemming as much from analysing and comparing prices, quality and service as from the accumulation of goods themselves.

One of a number of female characters in *Fortunata y Jacinta* who subvert the ideological divide of public and private space, Barbarita combines a voracious appetite for shopping with her family role as wife and mother. Charnon-Deutsch argues, for example, that in nineteenth-century Spain, 'the private woman, the humble servant of God, family, and spouse, reigned (morally if not economically) supreme in the home, but was clearly out of place in the street where she was nevertheless required to venture to make purchases or attend Mass'.[14] Barbarita leaves the family home regularly to do both, but she never seems 'out of place'. Shopping is a daily event: 'There were days when the purchases were big, and days when they were small, but there were never days when there were none at all. If she didn't need anything basic, the luxuriant lady brought home gloves, safety pins, metal cleanser, a package of hair pins, or whatever else had struck her fancy at a penny bazaar' (*FJ*, 95). It is attendance at Mass, moreover, that provides both Barbarita and Isidora with an ostensible purpose for their 'window shopping'. Isidora visits the Iglesia de San Luis, dreaming throughout the service of a future of riches and luxury, fully aware that she can linger before her journey home in the shopping streets clustered around the Puerta del Sol. Estupiñá whispers the daily offers of the market to Barbarita under cover of prayer in the pews at San Ginés, where it is not God but partridge, veal, salmon or lobster that is worshipped as 'divine, really divine' (*FJ*, 93). The replacement of religious devotion with the worship of the commodity is as evident as in cities where department stores were defining themselves as the new 'cathedrals' of consumption.

A number of large stores sprung up in Madrid in the second half of the nineteenth century that, although modest in size and diversity of goods, did introduce 'modern' retailing practices and services. Mesonero Romanos, for example, informs us that 'vast numbers of all types of shops cluster in every part of Madrid' [se encuentran en Madrid en todas partes infinidad de tiendas de géneros de toda especie], giving the city 'an exceptional liveliness' [una animacion singular].[15] The principal concentration of luxury establishments, tailors and jewellers, centered around the Puerta del Sol, on the calles de Montera, Carretas, San Jeronimo and del Carmen, and in the arcades (*pasajes*) of Del Iris and Nueva Galeria. Mesonero also notes a number of 'elegantly adorned department stores, served by skilful assistants'.[16] These typically remained family businesses, however, catering for a select clientele, such as Sobrino Brothers, mentioned in *La desheredada*, *La de Bringas* and *Fortunata y Jacinta*, which traded in silks and drapery. Barbarita Santa Cruz, for example, regularly patronises Sobrino's and gourmet shops such as Pla's and Gallo's, as well as the high-quality market stalls and butchers of the Plaza Mayor and penny bazaars. By the 1880s, however, European-style grand department stores or *grandes almacenes* had begun to spring up in the city. The De la Unión on the Calle de Mayor and the Exposicion Comercial on the Calle de Carretas both advertised free entry and fixed pricing, offering a very different retail experience to a more general customer.[17]

Towards the end of *Fortunata y Jacinta*, Galdós depicts the opening of a mammoth store, the brainchild of Samaniego, an astute haberdasher, and financed by the urbane, anglophile banker Don Mañuel Moreno-Isla. Managed by Samaniego's daughter Aurora, a widow who has returned to Madrid from Bordeaux, the shop sells garments and fabrics ordered directly from Paris and epitomises the influence of cosmopolitan modernity:

> The project was huge. Aurora would be in charge of trousseaux, christening, children's and ladies apparel. . . . The shop was to be in a new building near Santa Cruz square, facing Pontejos, and its window displays were sure to be the most glamorous and elegant in Madrid. (*FJ*, 633)

As in *Au Bonheur des Dames*, the store's bourgeois future clientele await the opening with greedy eagerness, and during the long nightly conversations between Aurora, her mother and Doña Lupe, 'their only subject was the new business and the unconceived wonders that Madrid's elegant society would admire there' (*FJ*, 634).

Describing preparations for the opening, including the installation of gas lighting, Aurora enthuses:

> It's going to be splendid. Shipments are already arriving and there are things that are so pretty there's nothing to match them in all Madrid. They just don't know how to do shop windows here. Wait till you see ours – full of the nicest things you can find. They'll catch people's eye and make them stop and come in to buy. Once they're in we'll show them more; we'll make them see things at different prices and they'll end up falling for the best. Shopkeepers here hardly know what the art of *étalage* is, and as for the art of selling – few have that. (*FJ*, 634)

Offering chic, exotic goods, and following European innovations in window-dressing, grand façades, and well-lit and luxurious interiors, the shop is a rapid success:

> Seldom had a business in Madrid been so full of life or shown clearer signs that it had impressed and appealed to the public. The exquisite novelties that Pepe Samaniego had brought from Paris attracted crowds of people; ladies swarmed around and quickly stuck to the honey. (*FJ*, 648)

Trained in the art of seductive display, Aurora applies her professional skills in the art of selling and dress as much to the creation of her own sophisticated image as an 'elegant working woman' (*FJ*, 634) as to the shop, carefully capitalising upon her respectable and independent position as a widow and committed working woman. Her success in securing the attentions of Juanito Santa Cruz away from Fortunata reflects the captivation of the bourgeois consumer by the beguiling Samaniego store, and further illustrates the power of European influence in the aspiring modern city. For if *La desheredada* reveals a culture of shopping associated with modernity and bourgeois femininity in 1860s Madrid, the opening of the Samaniego store in *Fortunata y Jacinta* heralds a new era of spectacular consumption.

Galdós's response to the consumer scene is largely ambivalent. It is the entice-ment of an exquisite shawl in Sobrino's, for example, that stirs Rosalía's latent passion for finery in *La de Bringas* and initiates her downward slide into debt, deception and adultery. The shop is repeatedly described by Galdós as 'evil' and a 'temptation', and Sobrino himself is shown luring his client to the latest fashions and fabrics with 'devilish amiability' (*B*, 155). Unlike her spendthrift and insolvent aristocratic friend the Marquesa de Tellería, Rosalía is naturally a careful shopper. She makes her own clothes from offcuts of fabric, and, when she does buy something, will 'think it over for a long time first and agonise over the cost' (*B*, 33), before always paying in cash. Sobrino's, however, offers the possibility of buying on credit, a service commonplace from the eighteenth century as it facilitated aristocratic patronage. As Galdós describes in his account of the cloth trade in *Fortunata y Jacinta*: 'Competition got tougher every year, and they had to think up new ways to attract steady customers, to receive and send out buyers, to pamper the clientele, and to let the steady customers, especially the female ones, open long-term accounts' (*FJ*, 12). By the middle of the nineteenth century, and the rise of a new bourgeois consumer, credit also provided middle-class women with an immediate purchasing power that they did not technically possess; a system that encouraged spending yet at the same time was fraught with financial liability for the retailer, provoking social and legal anxiety across Europe.

If Isidora and Rosalía's impulsive spending and love of luxury casts them as selfish and destructive, it thus also reveals the gendered power dynamics of an economic system in which women rarely have any independent financial control. Each enjoys the power of buying whatever they like, but their access to goods is ultimately dependent on male support, whether that of husband, paying lover or money-lender. Both Isidora and Rosalía, in order to satisfy their desire for commodities, must necessarily become commodities themselves if they are to finance their purchases or pay off their debts. The impressionable female shopper, buying voraciously and at whim on credit, and running up debts that her husband could not or would not pay, was an image of public concern in the social, media, legal and business literatures of the day, thoughtlessly destroying both the retailer and her own family. Isidora's reckless spending in the first part of *La desheredada*, for example, is paralleled by the steady pawning and selling of her possessions and her body in the second. And when Rosalía, although frightened by the exorbitant price of the shawl, finally gives in to the temptation of credit, she starts a pattern of purchasing and borrowing that she cannot finance, a 'logic . . . born in the jolting of a carriage that took her from shop to shop under the intoxicating influence of an overdose of fripperies' (*B* 38). Rosalía is a vain, envious and silly woman, and a character for whom Galdós spares little sympathy, although her ultimate moral degradation is depicted as resulting as much from the corruptions of consumer society as from her own weakness.

The Urban Spectacle

Philippe Hamon describes the nineteenth-century city as 'given over to the euphoric exercise of the gaze', in which society 'perceives its surroundings as a series of juxtaposed spectacles or a collection susceptible to comfortable visual inspection'.[18] Madrid was no exception, and for wealthy and middle-class society the city was a space of spectacle. Cafés such as El Suizo and El Fornos catered to an aristocratic and upper bourgeois clientele in opulent surroundings decorated with mirrors, perfect for self-display as much as for dining, the ultimate in luxury being the café-restaurant Lhardy, its French patisserie and haute cuisine the mark of upper-class, Europeanised sophistication. Along with the *paseo*, the pleasure garden, the circus, the opera and the theatre, they were places to see and be seen.

Madrid did not possess a public park until after the revolution of 1868, when the new provisional government dedicated the royal gardens of the Parque del Retiro to the population of the city, with the decree that its area was to be used exclusively for purposes of recreation and instruction. As in other European capitals, the provision of green spaces was regarded as an important antidote to the unhealthy conditions of urban life, providing recreation and relaxation, and encouraging the physical and moral edification of the working-class populace, whilst presenting a pleasant environment for leisured display on the part of the social elite. The Retiro combined a variety of roles in a space that mixed all levels of society. The Paseo de Carruajes (Carriage Parade), for example, a wide avenue with side promenades for riders and pedestrians, was the fashionable rendezvous of high society. So too were the open-air concerts of classical and contemporary music by the orchestras of the Sociedad de Conciertos (1866–1903) and the Unión Artístico-Musical (1877–1891). The refreshment kiosks and cafés, ice-rink, zoo, and regattas and firework displays on the Grand Lake, however, attracted a broader social audience, as well as the itinerant salesmen, paupers and other figures of the *demi-monde* that accompany concentrations of people at leisure. Of the zoo, in particular, the journal *La Ilustración de España* wrote in 1886, 'on Spring mornings and afternoons, people from all walks of madrileñian society gather there, before or after visiting the leafy and cheerful gardens of the Park' [en primavera, por las mañanas y tardes, se reunen allí todas las clases sociales de Madrid, antes o después de ir a las frondosas alamedas y sonrientes jardines del Parque].[19]

During the heat of high summer, when the wealthy traditionally vacated to a more temperate climate, the Retiro became the retreat of the middle classes. For Galdós's Rosalía de Bringas, to remain in Madrid over the summer is a tortuously boring experience, and above all an embarrassing admission of financial inadequacy in the eyes of society:

A fine summer she was going to have, lonely, bored to tears, sweltering to death, putting up with the rudest and most tiresome of husbands, and undergoing, in short, the shame of staying in Madrid when even concierges and boarding-house owners were going away for the summer! To have to say 'We didn't go anywhere this summer' was a declaration of struggling gentility that the aristocratic lips of a daughter of the Pipaóns and Calderón de la Barcas, of an illustrious scion of a whole dynasty of Palace officials, simply refused to pronounce. (*B*, 132–3)

In the bourgeois world of the mid-nineteenth century, however, the social tone was changing, Galdós himself, for example, stating in 1865 that 'the Court leaves and Madrid remains unchanged, with its polite society, its artists and literati, its insatiable thirst for spectacle, its uncontrolled appetite for diversion, and its constant gossip-mongering' [la Corte se marcha y Madrid se queda lo mismo que estaba, con su buena sociedad, sus artistas, sus literatos, su insaciable sed de espectáculos, su desordenado apetito de diversiones y su inalterable chismografía].[20] Although the Retiro was not open to public use until after 1868, spaces of diversion were nevertheless provided by a multitude of open-air theatres and public pleasure gardens, typically open from mid-spring until the end of summer. The earliest, such as the Jardín de las Delicias at the northern end of the Paseo de Recoletos, appeared after the decree of disentailment in 1834, offering relatively modest amusements such as refreshments, firework displays and dances. By the 1860s, however, Recoletos had become a concentrated amusement zone, dominated by open-air theatres, circuses and pleasure gardens.

A specifically nineteenth-century and initially middle-class phenomenon, the pleasure garden yet quickly became extremely popular with both the bourgeoisie and the aristocracy. Rafael Botella's painting of a grand ball in the Jardines del Paraíso in 1862 (Fig. 3), for example, portrays what appears to be an almost entirely bourgeois scene. The majority of men wear the black coats and long hats described by Galdós in his summary of Spanish fashion at the beginning of *Fortunata y Jacinta*. The women are likewise in full crinolines of fairly muted colour, with only one, to the right of the picture, wearing a bright red manila shawl. The atmosphere, moreover, is unequivocally respectable, with children taking part in the dancing, one woman carrying a small baby, and another couple accompanied by their dog. The largest amusement park, the Campos Elíseos, offered more spectacular and titillating entertainments, and drew a distinguished audience. Opening in 1864, it included a circular plaza with a capacity for 30,000 people, its own theatre (the Teatro Rossini), a bull ring, several cosmoramas and dioramas, the rollercoaster-style 'russian mountain', a boating river, shooting range, bathing house and equestrian ring, and became a regular feature of Galdós's articles for the *Revista de Madrid*. 'There the most elegant ladies of Madrid shine in all their splendour' [Allí brillan en todo su esplendor las damas más elegantes de Madrid], he described in 1865, 'a vast and magical group, an ensemble of crêpe, flowers, crinoline and feathers' [un inmenso grupo fantástico, conjunto de gasa, flores, crinolina y plumas].[21] The social crowd of Botella's painting seem sedate in comparison to the scene Galdós observes in the Campos Elíseos, a lavish yet disordered spectacle 'in which a thousand fans flutter, in which the coloured bands

Figure 3 Rafael Botella, *El Jardin publico de Madrid llamado 'El Paraíso' en noche de baile* (1862), Museo Municipal de Madrid

that adorn heads seem to intersect like the lights of a kaleidoscope, in which bouquets of flowers pass from hand to hand and scandalous words from mouth to mouth' [en que mil abanicos se agitan, en que se ven cruzar como las luces de un kaleidóscopo las cintas de colores que adornan las cabezas, en que los ramos de flores pasan de mano en mano y las palabras incendiarias de boca en boca], and that he complains 'leads the imagination astray and produces a type of vertigo or bewilderment' [extravia la imaginacion y produce una especie de vértigo ó atolondramiento].[22]

Occupying a large area of over 1,300 square feet to the north of the Retiro, the Campos Elíseos eventually gave way to the encroaching Barrio de Salamanca in 1881, and the Jardines del Buen Retiro, which opened in 1876 to the west of the main park, overlooking the Plaza de Cibeles, thus took over the role as the playground of Madrid society. Pío Baroja remembered the gardens during the social season of June and early July as a 'great gala' [gran gala], in which the famous figures of Madrid high and theatrical society were on display.[23] Spaces of leisure and entertainment, a broad spectrum of the Madrid population converged in the gardens in a way that they did not in the winter months. On the relative cool of a high summer evening, Baroja informs, one could expect to see impoverished aristocratic families remaining in the city, politicians, journalists and other professionals, along with members of the small commercial, artisan and labouring classes. 'The spectacle', he states, 'was exclusively madrileñian, somewhat aristocratic, somewhat provincial, elegant and at the same time excessively poor' [El espectáculo era exclusivamente madrileño, un tanto cortesano, un tanto provinciano, elegante y al mismo tiempo pobretón].[24] *Las noches del Buen Retiro* (*Nights in the Retiro Gardens*), Baroja's elegy to the Madrid belle époque written from the distance of 1934, depicts a society that is past, finally caught up by modernity and mass culture.[25]

The fascinated disapproval with which Galdós describes high society at play, anticipates his depiction of the affluent display of the new landscape of the east of the city in *La desheredada*. In Isidora Rufete, Galdós created a modern female protagonist who may be conceited and shallow, but who is also skilfully conversant in the rhetoric of spectacular consumerist urbanity. Shortly after arriving in Madrid, her social vanity already evident, Isidora takes a Sunday excursion to the Prado and Retiro with the medical student Augusto Miquis. Relaxing in the park, however, her attention is quickly caught by the contrast of her unsophisticated appearance with the spectacle of wealthy society around her. Obsessed with the elegant luxury of a world to which she is keenly aware she does not belong, she dislikes the zoo, claiming it is merely 'a spectacle for the common people' (*D*, 61). As Miquis walks Isidora home, they pass the site where the new bourgeois district of Salamanca is under construction:

> They went down into gullies where the soil was sown with sparse, stunted corn; they climbed up to the dumping grounds where slowly, as the earth was removed in Municipal carts, new streets were being laid out; they passed close by the rag-dealers' huts, built from planks, broken doors or matting and armour plated with sheets made from old oil cans; they stopped to watch small boys and chickens poking about in the straw. (*D*, 65)

Over the meagre and crude ground is being built the hard and ordered surface of a modern city of asphalt. Madrid, like its newly bourgeois public, is a city that is reinventing itself, engaged in the urban renovations that will transform it from a provincial capital into a modern metropolis, and disavowing those who will have no place within it. The *Ensanche* did not require the full-scale destruction of the city centre demanded by Haussman in Paris, but it was based on similar principles of social order: categorisation and exclusion.

Finally they reach the urban artery of the Paseo de la Castellana, surging with elite society on display. The Castellana, lined with open-air cafés, restaurants and entertainment booths, was from its development in 1854 the city's most fashionable avenue. Miquis describes the parade of carriages, with good-humoured disgust, as 'a torrent of vanity' (*D*, 71). Later in the novel, as eminent doctor and

Galdós's voice of institutional middle-class society, Miquis will assume the role of Isidora's moral custodian, and it is thus ironic that it is he who now explains to her the principles of imitation and illusion on which she will base her future:

> You'll see all social classes here. They come to be observed, to be compared and to see the respective distances between each other, in order to prepare for the assault. It's a case of climbing up the next run on the ladder. . . . They all rub shoulders and are tolerant of each other because equality rules over all. Nobody envies an illustrious name, but they do envy material possessions. As each one is furiously determined to go up in the world, he begins by posing. These improvisations stimulate the appetite. (*D*, 74)

Exhilarated by the spectacle of the Castellana, a decorative gala which Baroja would recall resembled the 'spiritual effeminisation of a Watteau landscape' [afeminamiento espiritual de un pasaje de Wateau], Isidora ignores the implicit critique in Miquis' commentary.[26] Responding only to the materiality of the fashionable nobility, she is overwhelmed by the city's allure:

> Her whole heart and mind were swept along on the swell. Far in the distance quite a few gas lights were shining through the dust of the Prado. That mist that forms from the breath of the city population, the evaporation from sprinkling water and the continual sweeping (the trains of dresses acting as brooms), was being illuminated into a fantastic glow, like a luminous radiation from the ground itself. (*D*, 75)

Just as Galdós's imagination was disoriented by the kaleidoscopic opulence of the Campos Elíseos, so Isidora's is beguiled by the incandescence of Madrid at dusk. Her fantastical illusion, Galdós implies, is also the writer's own.

Perhaps Galdós most overt critique of Madrid's collective artifice is voiced by another of his regular cast, Refugio Sánchez Emperador, in *La de Bringas*:

> Madrid's all show, you know. A gentleman I know says that this place is a sort of ongoing carnival, where the poor dress as rich people. In this city, everyone's poor, barring the odd few. It's all sham, ma'am, pure sham. People here don't live comfortably at home. They live in the street; there are families who survive all year round on nothing but potato omelettes just so they can dress well and go to the theatre . . . I know women whose husbands are civil servants who are out of work half the year, and you wouldn't believe how beautifully turned out they are. They look like duchesses and their children like royalty. How do they do it? I have no idea. A gentleman I know says that Madrid is full of mysteries like that. (*B*, 169)

Part of a Madrilenian *demi-monde*, turning up in the various guises of artist's model, revolutionary, courtesan, and *tertulia* hostess, Refugio is a rather bizarre yet perceptive commentator on Madrid society. In *La de Bringas* she has been attempting to set herself up in the fashion trade, dealing in luxury goods sent from France by her sister, who has previously eloped with a wealthy relative of Rosalía. When Rosalía swallows her hypocritical moral pride and visits Refugio to beg for a loan at the end of the novel, the business has failed, partly due to constant exploitation by wealthy customers such as Rosalía herself. Enjoying her moment of power, Refugio taunts her visitor with a lecture on the bankruptcy of Madrid's entire social spectacle. 'A gentleman friend of mine', she repeats, making no attempt to hide her easy relations with men, 'says that there's nothing but shabbiness all round; that there are no real aristocrats here, and that almost all the so-called rich people, the high society types, are nobodies' (*B*, 170). Attacking the self-righteous yet empty morals of the upper-classes with revolutionary fervour, she declares, 'I don't owe anyone anything, and if I do, I pay up; I work for my living, and no one can tell me what to do, and most of all I'm not trying to pull the wool over anyone's eyes; if people don't like me the way I am, they can lump it. (*B*, 171)

Isidora, by contrast, has no intention of working for a living, and in his description of the pseudo-luxury of the Castellana, Miquis unwittingly hands her what is effectively a conduct manual. The cause of her subsequent overspending is not merely a greedy desire for possessions. It is more fundamentally a desire for identity. Rather like the new city itself, springing up from the dust of demolition and expansion, Isidora has detached herself from her provincial past, yet, at the same time, her new sense of self requires consolidation. The goods she buys are the trivial luxuries of fashion that symbolise and convey the outward impression of a social status that she does not possess. Her dependency on material appearance for her sense of self, and on the narratives of mass consumer culture for her attitudes and actions, implies a questioning of any simple definition of identity, one that moves beyond the familiar narrative of the shallow female protagonist whose vanity and material desires lead to a life of empty consumerism, moral degeneration and death.

Rachel Bowlby argues that in the world of consumer capitalism, '[t]he commodity makes the person and the person is, if not for sale, then an object whose value or status can be read off with accuracy in terms of the things he has and the behavioural codes he adopts'.[27] As Elizabeth Kowaleski-Wallace states, moreover, 'Shopping is not just about appetite; it is about projection, fantasy, and desire'.[28] In a society in which commodities and the principle of spectacle become constitutive of identity, Isidora consumes in order to create herself in the image of the wealthy women she sees on the Castellana and indeed believes herself to be. Isidora excels in exactly this approximation of an identity through commercial accummulation, but in her desperate need for the objects that will sustain that identity, ultimately becomes a figure who is indeed herself for sale. The street for Isidora is the space of both her dreams and her disillusionment.

In contrast to older women such as Barbarita or Guillermina who possess a placed relationship with Madrid, either through memory and association or regular activity, both Isidora and Fortunata Rubín in *Fortunata y Jacinta* are unequivocally represented as placeless, or rather out of place, in the city. Neither finds a permanent home and both move residence constantly, their changing abodes reflecting their changing fortunes. Fortunata, for example, although born and bred in the area of the Plaza Mayor and possessing an innate knowledge of Madrid *viejo* similar to that of Barbarita, is passively moved about the city according to the various demands and whims of her husband, his family and her various lovers; from the Calle de Pelayo in the heart of Madrid *viejo*, to the reform convent of the Micaelas, the Rubín married home on the Calle de Sagunto in Chamberí, the apartment rented for her by Juanito Santa Cruz in Cuatro Caminos on the northern outskirts of the city, another rented by her elderly paramour Don Evaristo Feijóo on the calle de Tabernillas, back to the Rubín family home, by this time Ave María Street, until she finally returns to the Calle de Pelayo to die in childbirth. Every one of these shifts of location is orchestrated by others, Fortunata seemingly having no agency over her place within the city. Like Gautier's last *manola*, she embodies a *castizo* Madrid cast adrift and struggling to survive within the bourgeois city. Isidora's constant shifts of address similarly mark her fluctuating financial status and moral decline, as she moves from the house of her uncle Relimpio, near the Calle Hernán Cortés, again in an older area of the city, to the modern house in which she is set up by Joaquín Pez at the far end of the extending Calle Hortaleza, the Calle de las Huertas where she is contained as the mistress of the wealthy and controlling Sanchéz Botín, the Calle de los Abades in the working-class area in the south, and finally to the new Model Prison, where she is encarcerated for forging documents supporting her claim to the Aransis inheritance. If Fortunata is the eroticised personification of the city's fascinating and disappearing urban past, Isidora represents its self-delusive pretension to urban modernity.

Although Galdós's painstaking record of his unruly female protagonists' numerous places of residence fixes them within the order of street names and house numbers, it also serves to emphasise the lack of importance of such mapped space for the two young women themselves. Both Fortunata and Isidora spend much of their time making long journeys through the city, often when they are confused or disoriented. In the dramatisation of their receptive perceptual sensitivity and excitable imaginations, Galdós explores a new mode of female urban consciousness. When the pampered Juanito Santa Cruz breaks with Fortunata for the second time, for example, she is at first determinedly driven by her anger to confront him at home. On setting out, Galdós makes clear, her mind is resolute, indicated by her swift and direct movement through the city. 'She must not have been very upset', he explains, 'when instead of taking Montera (where the crowds slowed traffic) she headed for Salud Street in hopes of gaining ten minutes' (*FJ*, 480). Fortunata's ingrained knowledge of the city streets, however, disappears dramatically when she comes to a halt outside the Santa Cruz residence, suddenly paralysed by fear, shame and confusion. Her mental fever is evoked by her changed relationship with the city around her; she is 'distracted', walks 'mechanically', and is 'carried along by her own steps', unable to find her way home (*FJ*, 482). Wandering deliriously in the Puerta del Sol, she is approached by numerous men who assume she is a prostitute, before finally being recognised by the kindly Don Evaristo, who takes her home as she wildly proclaims her decency.

Isidora makes a similarly frenzied journey after the Marquesa de Aransis rejects her claim to family inheritance. Walking into a Madrid that is suddenly unfamiliar to her, turned to rubble by the contradiction of her fantasies, in her confused mind there has been a '[t]otal transformation. The world was quite different. Nature itself, the air and the light, all quite different' (*D*, 213). In what is one of the more subjective sequences of the novel, Galdós represents her disorientated response to the city as she moves aimlessly, then more meditatively, through its streets. Her trajectory at first takes her from the ugly Aransis palace in San Pedro, along the Calle de Segovia and Calle Mayor, to the Plaza de Oriente, a city built by the seventeenth-century Court and in which, her grand presumptions now destroyed, she no longer belongs. Isidora's desire for nobility, however, is never really much more than a desire for access to the pleasures of urban modernity, and, turning away from the aristocratic society of old Madrid that has denounced her, she walks towards the Puerta del Sol: 'As she drew closer to the centre of Madrid and felt the throbbing vitality of the city, the idea of living grew even stronger within her: she wanted to experience, to see, to taste' (*D*, 218). Moving quickly to where '[t]he Puerta del Sol, beating like a heart permanently stimulated, revealed its fast moving breathless life' her excitement increases:

> Madrid, at eight thirty in the evening, is pure enchantment, an open market, a display of delights and endless pleasures. The theatres attract with their gas lit signs, the shops draw attention with the persuasive humbug of the window displays, the cafés fascinate with their buzz of conversation and casual atmosphere, where sweet idleness and gossip flourish. Wandering about at this time of the evening has all the attractions of a stroll and the seductions of a journey into the unknown. (*D*, 219)

The mass of people is greater than usual, and she tingles with postive energy, 'excited by the endless repeated impressions of the jostling, brushing, pushing crowd, of things seen and desired' (*D*, 220). King Amadeo has abdicated, the Republic been declared, and the city suddenly seems a place of possibility. Caught up both physically and emotionally by the crowd surging towards the Congreso on the Carrera de San Jerónimo, she exclaims at, 'How many men there were, and women too!', exhilarated by '[c]ontact with the masses, that fluid magnetic conductor of mysterious desires which flows from one body to another' (*D*, 221). Sol is an ambiguous site, however, at once a public arena where the new Republic is being shouted from one man to another, and a phantasmagoria of 'enchantment', 'display' and 'idleness' by which the frivolous Isidora is easily seduced. In the shop windows, '[a]s Carnival time was getting close, it was all masks, disguises and carnival heads . . . a façade of leering grimaces' (*D*, 220). The eve of the Republic is as portentous of folly as it is of equality. Isidora is blind to the paradoxical fact that her social aspirations, at the same time as they uphold a belief in aristocratic culture and elite taste, are in fact dependent on the possibility of class mobility. She has little genuine sympathy with ideas of collective equality, and her immediate act is to seek out the affections of Joaquín Pez and the promise of quick personal advancement, a prediction of the similar disintegration of the new Republic into a self-interested seizing of economic and political spoils.

Isidora's narrative of desire, extravagance and fall in the Spanish capital, accords with anxieties about mass urban modernity that were common across Western Europe more generally. The social, political, psychological and cultural discourse of the later nineteenth century, Andreas Huyssen argues, 'consistently and obsessively genders mass culture and the masses as feminine'.[29] Moreover '[t]he lure of mass culture', he continues, 'has been traditionally described as the threat of losing oneself in dreams and delusions and of merely consuming rather than producing'.[30] Galdós's modern Madrid is a city that consumes voraciously yet produces almost nothing, obsessed only with material appearance and social status. Just as Fortunata personifies a traditional and simple Madrid, passively moulded and destroyed by bourgeois society, Isidora too is thus presented by Galdós as an analogue of the city; epitomising a very male and bourgeois myth of the over-reaching ambition, self-delusion and corruption of mass culture.

Galdós's novels abound in the spatial configurations and practices of bourgeois Madrid; the systematised expansion and circulatory networks envisioned by the new liberal order, alongside the pedestrian eloquence, local vernacular and affectual epistemologies of the numerous people traversing the city in everyday life. He may never have relinquished his desire to capture the 'entire perspective' of the city streets, but he came to recognise their heterogeneity and transitivity. If the model of Madrid that Galdós chooses for *Fortunata y Jacinta* is a successful mercantile family, in *La desheredada* it is the lunatic asylum on the outskirts of the city at Leganés. 'Oh Leganés!' the narrator exclaims after hearing the delusions and fantasies of its inmates, '[i]f anyone wished to represent you in a theoretical city . . . there would be no architects or physiologists who would dare to mark in your hospitable walls' (*FJ*, 11). Madrid, likewise, Galdós implies, cannot be fixed by the architecture of urban planning or the physiologies of the writer. Madrid is a city formed by the convergence of flesh and stone, memory and myth, materiality and performance, delusion and fantasy.

−4−

City of Contrasts

From the perspective of the Plaza de Oriente, wrote Vicente Blasco Ibáñez in *La horda* (1905), Madrid 'looked like an imposing capital city, a major metropolis' [parecía una capital portentosa, una importante metrópoli].[1] During the first decade of the Restoration, guided by the authoritarian and repressive conservatism of prime minister Cánovas del Castillo, Spain experienced a period of political stability, economic confidence and bourgeois prosperity. Madrid was again required to reflect and express the values of a new regime, and the end of the nineteenth century witnessed a monumentalising of the urban landscape that showcased the grandeur and authority of the triumphant monarchy. Development was predominantly concentrated along the Paseos del Prado, de Recoletos and Castellana, with the *Ensanche* also receiving renewed support, with more concerted expansion of the district of Salamanca, and the rapid and extensive growth of northern suburbs additional to the original Castro plan, such as Chamberí and Argüelles. Confirming the relocation of power and wealth from the traditionally aristocratic west of the city to the institutional and commercial hegemony of its eastern strip, was a lavish programme of civic building, including the completion of the Biblioteca Nacional and Museo Arqueológico (1892), begun under the reign of Isabel II, the construction of a new building for the Ateneo (1884), and the building of the imposing headquarters of the Banco de España (1891), the Bolsa (the stock exchange, 1893), and the Ministerio de Agricultura (1897), all in the architectural style of eclectic classicism characteristic of Second Empire Paris.

If classical monumentalism was the favoured style of official and state buildings, construction in iron and glass, as elsewhere in Europe, became the emblem of functional architecture; notably for market buildings, and for the railway stations of Delicias (1880), Del Norte (1888) and Atocha (1892). Espousing industrial and technological progress in their very existence as much as in their purpose, these yet peculiarly diaphanous buildings formed a distinctive architectural aesthetic of metropolitan modernity. The Restoration city's practice of triumphalist self-display was perhaps epitomised, however, by the very *un*utilitarian Palacio de Cristal, designed by Ricardo Velázquez Bosco as an exhibition hall for the Exposición de Filipinas in 1887. Reminiscent of the design if not scale of Sir Joseph Paxton's Crystal Palace of 1851, the glass and iron structure of the Palacio de Cristal embodied national optimism and technological progress, ebulliently yet ironically proclaiming an imperial might that would be on the point of collapse within a decade. Spectacularly transparent in form, it yet ostentatiously masked economic crisis and massive social difference. The complacent viewpoint enjoyed by the city's social elite was self-absorbed and apathetic. For Baroja the aristocracy, wealthy bourgeoisie and social climbers of the Restoration city were at best greedy, callous and superficial, oblivious to the apalling poverty experienced by the majority of the population.

The Sociological Eye

Although Madrid's population had risen relatively slowly during the first half of the nineteenth century, from roughly 200,000 to 280,000, it boomed to almost 400,000 by the late 1870s, rising again to nearly 600,000 by 1910.[2] Much of the demographic increase was due to migration from the provinces, as mortality rates in the city were higher than in any other European capital, with 40 per cent of children dying before the age of five.[3] Most immigrants lived in conditions of extreme poverty, clustered in the working class *barrios* of Latina and Inclusa to the south of the city centre, or in slum areas springing up on the very outskirts of the city; Cuatro Caminos, Guindalera and Prosperidad, for example, well beyond the Ensanche to the north of the city, or Injurias, Embajadores and Peñuelas in the south. By the last decades of the century living conditions in these areas were abominable, outbreaks of cholera in 1885 and 1890, and tuberculosis in the first years of the twentieth century, provoking municipal concern. In April 1898 the city hosted the Ninth International Congress of Hygiene and Demography, which raised civic awareness of issues of sanitation, pollution and disease amongst the poorer classes. Detailed surveys into the health and living conditions of the urban population, notably by Austrian doctor Philiph Hauser, and César Chicote, director of the Laboratorio Químico Municipal, revealed the extent of the problem: massive unemployment due to agricultural and industrial depression, substandard and insalubrious accommodation, typically lacking running water, light or ventilation, filthy and polluted streets, no schooling, a meagre diet, the foodstuffs of the markets dirty, rotten or rancid.[4] Anxious debate over the effects on physical, moral and economic health of society as a whole ensued, yet little direct action. The Madrid authorities had few effective legislative solutions for the mediation of the city's social problems, and it would not be until 1911 that a bill was passed ordering the construction of cheap housing for the labouring classes.

'Madrid is surrounded by suburbs where a world of beggars, wretches and outcasts lives in worse conditions than in the depths of Africa' [Madrid está rodeado de suburbios, en donde viven peor que en el fondo de Africa un mundo de mendigos, de miserables, de gente abandonada], Baroja wrote in 1903, denouncing the injustice and disregard of a society that was obsessed with viewing and looking yet turned a blind eye to the conditions of its slums:

> Who concerns themselves with them? Nobody, absolutely nobody. I myself have walked through Injurias and Cambroneras at night, mingled with the lowlife in the taverns of Peñuelas and the bars at Cuatro Caminos and on Andalucía Street. I have seen women cramped together in the cellars of the government offices and men thrown naked into cells. I have seen ragged street urchins crawl from caves in the hills of San Blas and watched as they devoured dead cats. . . . And nowhere have I seen anyone take a real interest in all this wretchedness and poverty.
>
> [¿Quién se ocupa de ellos? Nadie, absolutamente nadie. Yo he paseado de noche por las Injurias y las Cambroneras, he alternado con la golfería de las tabernas de las Peñuelas y los merenderos de los Cuatro Caminos y de la carretera de Andalucía. He visto mujeres amontonadas en las cuevas del Goberno Civil y hombres echados desnudos al calabozo. He visto golfos andrajosos salir gateando de las cuevas del cerillo de San Blas y les he contemplado cómo devoraban gatos muertos. . . . Y no he visto a nadie que se ocupara en serio de tanta tristeza, de tanta laceria].[5]

In direct contrast to the ostentatious luxury of the Castellana and Retiro, the outskirts of the city presented a scene that was miserable and sordid.

'A great city', the Chicago sociologist Robert Park declared in 1915,

> tends to spread out and lay bare to the public view in a massive manner all the characters and traits which are ordinarily obscured and suppressed in smaller communities. The city, in short, shows the good and evil in human nature in excess. It is this fact, more than any other which justifies the view that would make of the city a laboratory or clinic in which human nature and social processes may be most conveniently and profitably studied.[6]

With his trilogy of Madrid-based novels *La lucha por la vida* (*The Struggle for Life*), published in 1904, Baroja presented to bourgeois readers the most abject spaces and conditions of their city. As implied by the Darwinian title, the connecting theme of the three novels, *La busca* (*The Search*), *Mala hierba* (*Bad Grass*) and *Aurora roja* (*Red Dawn*), is that of struggle and survival amidst the harsh and conflictual habitat of the urban lower classes. Thinly focused on the semi-orphaned figure of Manuel Alcázar, his descent into an underworld of delinquency and petty crime, and maturation into a fully fledged member of bourgeois society, their plot is less interesting than the catalogue of social types, occupations and dwelling spaces that they detail with zealous fascination. The Madrid of *La lucha por vida* is a grim landscape, across which move the street-vendors, rag-pickers, beggars, vagabonds, urchins, thieves, prostitutes, gamblers, ex-soldiers returned from the colonies, prostitutes, confidence tricksters and multiplicity of other figures who make up the world of the poor and deracinated. A trained physician, in the trilogy Baroja approached the outskirts of Madrid with the empirical perspective of an ethnographer, recording the appearance of the environment and people of its slums with careful detail. Although ambivalent towards the medical profession, stating in his biography that his tuition at the University of Madrid had been so poor that it left him almost incompetent, the principles of medical science remained central to his social, moral and philosophical beliefs in the enlightened progress and regeneration of Spain as a nation. For Baroja, fiction could (and should) present a more accurate reflection of social reality than history, and the role of the novelist was to strive to this end. However, although more concerned with authentic representation and moral sincerity than with aesthetic style, the Madrid novels nevertheless owe as much to the naturalised models of degeneration that inflected social and scientific thinking across *fin-de-siècle* Europe, as to the supposed objectivity of science. Spaces of abjection, Baroja's raw and disturbing images of the slums are the product of precise observation but also an imagination familiar with the quasi-scientific discourses of anthropology, criminology and psychobiology.

Of the three novels of the trilogy, it is perhaps *La busca* that most overtly manifests Baroja's sociological impulse, exploring the various miserable spaces and moral depths of the city's indigent society. With an average monthly salary among the working-class of about 75 pesetas per month, and daily subsistence costs for a family of three just under 4 pesetas per day, the 10 to 25 peseta rent on the most basic accommodation in the inner districts of the city was unaffordable even for those in regular employment.[7] Cheaper housing could be found, often in the form of makeshift dwellings. Perhaps the most common living spaces in lower working-class Madrid, however, were the *casas de vecindad* or *corralas*, blocks of small tenement flats built around a shared central patio. Hauser records that at least 400 such buildings were in existence in 1903, the majority clustered in the poorest districts of Inclusa, Latina and Hospital, and their inhabitants predominantly 'of the labouring class, of casual workers, of wandering salesmen, of street sweepers and rag-pickers' [de la clase jornalera, de empleados cesantes, de vendedores ambulantes, de barrenderos y de traperos].[8]

Describing one such building in the district of Embajadores, the 'Corralón', where Manuel stays in chapter 2 of *La busca*, Baroja begins with a detailed description and analysis of the shoddy and asymmetrical architecture of the building. 'Each neighbour was allowed to use for their own purposes the section of balcony adjoining their house', he notes, concluding in sociological manner that, 'from the appearance of this balcony area it was possible to deduce the level of poverty or material comfort of each family, their interests and tastes' [a cada vecino quedaba para sus menesteres el trozo de galería que ocupaba su casa; por el aspecto de este espacio podía colegirse el grado de miseria o de relativo bienestar de cada familia, sus aficiones y sus gustos] (*LB*, 291). Some hang with flowers or vines, but the majority with dirty clothes and bedspreads, revealing 'a resigned, passive wretchedness, combined with both physical and moral impoverishment' [la miseria resignada y perezosa, unida al empobrecimiento orgánico y al empobrecemiento moral] (*LB*, 292). The appearance of the central patio is dirty and repugnant:

> useless junk was piled up in one corner, covered with sheets of zinc; there were filthy rags and rotten planks, rubble, bricks, roof tiles and baskets; an infernal mess. Each afternoon residents washed on the patio and, once finished, emptied their bowls onto the floor. These pools of water dried leaving white stains and streaks of blue from the indigo water.... when it rained ... an unbearable pestilence rose from the festering black water which flooded the patio.
>
> [en un ángulo se levantaba un montón de trastos inservibles, cubierto de chapas de cinc; se veían telas puercas y tablas carcomidas, escombros, ladrillos, tejas y cestos; un revoltijo de mil diablos. Todas las tardes algunas vecinas lavaban en el patio, y cuando terminaban su faena vaciaban los lebrillos en el suelo, y los grandes charcos, al secarse, dejaban manchas blancas y regueros azules de agua de añil.... cuando llovía ... se producía una pestilencia insoportable de la corrupción del agua negra que inundaba el patio]. (*LB*, 291)

The physical and moral debasement of the poor corresponds directly to their wretched living conditions. For the inhabitants of the Corralón, poverty leads to dissatisfaction, loss of determination, indolence and vice, degeneration becoming self-reproductive and endemic. There is none of the hopefulness here of Galdós or Dickens for the potential redemption of the lower classes in spirituality or comic vitality. Baroja is too aware of Darwinian science, and his literary aesthetic too close to that of evolutionary naturalism, to subscribe to what George Eliot described as 'the miserable fallacy that high morality and refined sentiment can grow out of harsh social relations, ignorance, and want'.[9]

The anxiety that the foul environment of the slums bred crime and delinquency was a topic of civic and popular debate in turn-of-the-century Madrid, pickpockets and thieves being a common feature of the streets of the old slums and city centre. As Daniel Pick demonstrates, however, in nineteenth-century discourse on deviancy, 'degeneration was increasingly seen by medical and other writers not as the social condition of the poor, but as a self-reproducing force; not the effect but the cause of crime, destitution and disease'.[10] Social-scientific studies in Madrid, for example, documented various categories of urban deviant, defined in terms of both social determinism and pathological disorder.[11] Similarly, the array of social reprobates that Baroja presents across the trilogy are also presented within the language of psychological and physiological degeneration. Although products of harsh necessity and a lack of education, the juvenile delinquents that Manuel associates with in *La busca* have become inured to a life of survival through violence, vice and malice. Corresponding to the assumptions of the criminal physiology of Cesare Lombroso, for example, the appearance of 'el Bizco', the leader of this gang of thieves and rogues, reveals his moral degeneration. According to Lombroso, the study of an individual's phrenology and physiognomy revealed the stage he had reached on the evolutionary scale from primitivism to civilisation. Those of savage appearance, denoted by the racialised characteristics of a sloping forehead, large jaw, high cheekbones, were 'born criminals'. Bizco's appearance, 'his narrow skull, strong jaw, snout-like features and fierce stare made him look disgustingly brutal and animal' [Su cráneo estrecho, su mandibula fuerte, su morro, la mirada torva, le daban un aspecto de brutalidad y animalidad repelentes] (*LB*, 301), along with the tattoo that covers his chest and arms, another of Lombroso's markers of savagery, epitomises that of the natural criminal, confirming his atavism.

Critics praised the *La lucha por vida* as a study of social description, and the writer Gregorio Marañon, speaking on Baroja's election to the Academia Española in 1935, argued that his novels provided 'a more exact and fundamental documentation of the Spain of our time' [una documentación más exacta y fundamental de la España de nuestro tiempo] than any social or historical records and accounts.[12] Yet to accept Baroja's description of himself as an 'impartial and truthful chronicler' [cronista imparcial y verídico] (*LB*, 264) at face value, and to read his novels and memoirs as documentary accounts of Madrid at the end of the nineteenth century, is to disregard the limits and contradictions of objective observation that he frequently alludes to in his writing. Despite the best classifying efforts of doctors and social scientists, the slum conditions and urban poor of Madrid's periphery evaded definition. As the examples of degradation and inertia in the Corralón, for example, continue to pile upon the senses of the narrator rather like its mountains of rubbish, they become increasingly overwhelming. Despite the occasional glimpse of a whitewashed wall or clean curtain, signalling a brave defiance of abjection, the majority of the scene is 'nauseating and repulsive' [nauseabunda y repulsivo] (*LB*, 292). The narrator's reaction is here physical and synaesthetic, the observing eye suddenly embodied in the multisensual overload of nausea. In response to the feeling of loathing incited by the materiality of the patio, Baroja distances himself through the signifying artifice of synecdoche and metaphor. The *corrala* is a world in itself, he states in classificatory desperation, a wretched 'microcosm' [micocosmos] of society. From the ostensibly objective and specific language of physiological and empirical science, he is forced into the abstractions of a more pseudoscientific discourse. The unruly expanse of the *corrala* is imaginatively reconstructed into a legible space, the immediate realities with which it confronts the narrator projected onto the broader (and more removed) social and philosophical questions of the condition of Spain more generally.

Ultimately, rather than providing an objective rendering of the environment of the city slums, the Madrid trilogy reveals and interrogates the ways in which their physical space becomes a connotative space of degeneration and abjection. The urban periphery becomes a site for the projection of Baroja's critique of the values of bourgeois capitalism, but also of broader fears and anxieties about working-class unrest, the collapse of colonial control, and the social, political and cultural degeneration of the nation as a whole. Stallybrass and White argue that nineteenth-century European cultures 'think themselves' through the high/low oppositions of four interconnected domains, 'psychic forms, the human body, geographical space and the social order'.[13] The elite society of Restoration Madrid defined itself by the exclusion and denial of all that contradicted its self-image of progress and modernity. Commenting on Western society's practices of pollution ritual and sanitation, Mary Douglas states that 'pollution behaviour is the reaction which condemns any object or idea likely to confuse or contradict cherished ideals'.[14] The slums are the social, spatial and symbolic location of modernity's 'other'; the waste that it produces yet finds loathsome. In *Mala hierba*, for example, the *barrio* of Injurias, presided over by the gasworks of the Fábrica de Gas, is 'infected' [infecto]:

> Some were rag-pickers; others, beggars; others, half-dead from hunger; almost all of them repulsive in appearance. The women looked even worse than the men, dirty, dishevelled, tattered. That revolting district spewed forth human refuse, wrapped in rags, numb with cold and damp.
> [algunos, traperos; otros, mendigos; otros, muertos de hambre; casi todos de facha repulsiva. Peor aspecto que los hombres tenían aún las mujeres, sucias, desgreñadas, haraposas. Era una basura humana, envuelta en guiñapos, entumecida por el frío y la humedad, la que vomitaba aquel barrio infecto]. (*MH*, 461)

The metonymic association of the *barrio* with contamination, the result of the social ills of industrial pollution and disease, yields here to metaphor. These men and women, engulfed in rags, dirty, impoverished and starving, are 'repulsive' because they embody and expose problems that the social order would prefer to reject. The nauseating refuse of the bourgeois city, they literally become the 'vomit' of the polluted slum.

Abject Impressionism

Baroja's Madrid novels present an empirical impression of life, rather than a mechanical reproduction of the external scene. Approaching Madrid by train at the beginning of *La busca*, Manuel's first view is of a menacing glow produced by the lights of the city centre, 'a red twilight climbing the sky, shot with blood like the pupil of a monster' [un crepúsculo rojo esclarecía el cielo, inyectado de sangre como la pupila de un monstruoso] (*LB*, 269), followed by the sight of the poor and sordid slums of the outskirts. The image depicts not so much the solid materiality of the city as the mood it produces in the mind of the observing Manuel, the combination of sense perception and subjectivity. Manuel may not be a strongly dramatised or psychologised character, but he is a keen receptor of the sensory impressions of the urban landscape. Waking one morning after sleeping rough, for example, he watches the break of dawn turn the city into a composition of forms and colours:

> Madrid, flat, pallid, bathed in humidity, jutted out into the night, its roof-tops cutting the sky in a straight line; its towers, its tall factory chimneys and, in the silence of daybreak, the town and the distant landscape, took on the ethereal, static quality of a painting . . . wrapped in the damp, cold and sadness of the morning, under a low, zinc-coloured sky. [Madrid, plano, blanquecino, bañado por le humedad, brotaba de la noche con sus tejados, que cortaban en un línea recta el cielo; sus torrecillas, sus altas chimineas de fábrica y, en el silencio del amanecer, el pueblo y el paisaje lejano tenían algo de lo irreal y de lo inmóvil de una pintura . . . todo envuelto en la atmósfera húmeda, fría y triste de la mañana, bajo un cielo bajo de color de cinc]. (LB, 343)

Baroja's vicarious fascination with the vagrancy of the homeless is here aesthetic rather than social. For Manuel, however, shivering with cold, the aesthetic shades and harmonies of the elemental landscape are unreal compared to the everyday experience of the slums.

'My heart is vagabond' [Mi corazón es vagabundo], Baroja once stated, and his self-identification with the figure of the vagrant is evident across his writing.[15] Through the character of Manuel he explores the liminal and nomadic identity of the urban itinerant. Constantly roaming the city, sleeping anywhere from the caves of Príncipe Pío and the corralas of Injurias, to the walls of the Plaza de Oriente and the benches of the Castellana, Manuel is a *golfo*, a term applied by social commentators at the turn of the century to a broad range of otherwise unidentifiable and placeless persons. Baroja devoted an entire article to this elusive figure, 'Patología del golfo' ('Pathology of the *golfo*') in 1900, in which he defines the *golfo* as the product of the contemporary city, those abandoned or disinherited, the waste and strays of society. The *golfo* is neither 'a thief, nor an idler, but a beggar' [un mendigo, ni un ratero, ni un desocupado], a parasite, of more or less destructive breed, who operates throughout the city, living off or at the expense of others, and who exists within all classes, from the poor to the aristocratic.[16] The concern of social commentators, and Baroja himself, to 'pathologise' the placeless *golfo* is clear, for he is the embodiment of a disconcertingly itinerant waste, refusing spatial abjection to the margins. At the same time, however, he is a reflection of the urban writer who wanders the city, detached from society, making the street and the café his home.

The nomadism of the rag-picker was at once more legitimate and more regulated than that of the *golfo*; he fulfilled a functional role, required an official licence, and as he only operated in the early hours of the morning (up to eight o'clock in summer and ten o-clock in winter), remained largely invisible to the prosperous inhabitants of the northern suburbs. Hauser estimates that there were over 10,000 registered ragmen operating in Madrid at the beginning of the twentieth century, collecting and transporting refuse in wagons pulled by mules or donkeys to the rubbish tips on the outskirts of the city.[17] Moving daily between north and south, east and west, between the elegance and wealth, filth and poverty of the city, the rag-picker traverses the social fixities of space and reverses their conventional values; transforming bourgeois Madrid into the space of the useless and unwanted, and taking waste objects to the urban periphery where they are endowed with new purpose and value. Señor Custodio, the cheerful old ragman in *La busca* who takes Manuel as his apprentice, possesses an expert knowledge of the city, his journeys instinctive, directed even in the dense fog of winter by a fixed and ingrained map. Painstakingly sorting and recycling waste, he sells empty bottles to breweries, wine stores and pharmacists, collects remnants of paper and rags for paper-mills, and saves vegetable scraps as food for his pigs and chickens. The rubbish of one part of the city becomes the subsistence of another, a 'crude and humble life sustained by the detritus of refined and luxuriant living' [vida tosca y humilde, sustenar con las detritus del vivir refinado y vicioso] (*LB*, 367), that Manuel thinks must be one of the happiest in the world. Of course there is an obvious difference of perspective between the Parisian phenomenon of the leisured *flâneur*, a strolling 'man about town', and the outcast tramps and delinquents of Baroja's Madrid. Yet there is a common sensibility between Benjamin's *flâneur* and the rag-picker that he describes as 'fascinating his epoch', an urban phenomenon within whom the writer 'could recognize a bit of himself'.[18] Through the fictional persona of Manuel and Señor Custodio, Baroja assumes the sensibility of the *flâneur* as conceived through Benjamin's surrealist gaze, roving the marginal and liminal areas of the bourgeois city of modernity, intoxicated by its phantasmagoric image even as he indicts the harshness, squalor, misery and injustice of its reality. In Baroja's use of the tropes of the *golfo* and the rag-picker in the trilogy, we find a self-reflexive exploration of his own vagrant *flânerie* and aesthetic transformation of waste.

The squalid living conditions that existed on the extreme margins of the city could remain relatively ignored by the geographically distant rich and middle classes of the Puerta de Alcalá and Barrio de Salamanca. The older and more central areas of the city, however, were socially and spatially more indefinite. The *golfo* and the rag-picker continually collapse the geographically delimited zones of wealth and poverty, city centre, suburbs and periphery, emphasising the economic interdependence of the affluent and deprived spaces of the city. As Madrid's urban infrastructure developed, the mutability of social-spatial boundaries became an increasing threat. New transport systems, initially geared towards the needs and demands of the affluent suburbs, reduced the physical, temporal and social distance between different urban areas, bringing into proximity spaces that had previously been more segregated. The inauguration of the first tramline in 1871, for example, connected the middle-class residential areas of Argüelles-Pozas and Salamanca with the commercial centre of the Puerta del Sol, but also the gaze of the urban poor. A short story by novelist Emilia Pardo Bazán illustrates the ways in which the tram offered a detached refuge from the realities beyond its window, facilitating the abstract separation of different locales, and yet was also a confined space in which any unfamiliar intrusion was particularly evident, thus disturbingly emphasising the realities of urban difference. 'En tranvía' ('In the Tram'), begins with a description of the bourgeois passengers taking a tram from the Puerta del Sol to Salamanca; women accompanied by elegant, beautifully dressed children, a nine-year old girl who crosses her legs and indolently swings an expensively shod foot, a complacent young pregnant woman, an arrogant matron pretending to sleep.[19] The narrator is another such wealthy passenger, enjoying the sun and serenity of this Sunday morning in early spring. Amidst the general feeling of abstract well-being, however, sits a woman from the pueblo, holding a sleeping child. Disturbed by this perturbing intrusion into an otherwise agreeable day, the narrator observes the woman curiously, and is shocked at the desperation on her face.

The Madrid tram in Pardo Bazán's tale operates as a self-contained space of bourgeois detachment from the chaos and crowds of the city. Moving from the commercial and social hubbub of the Puerta del Sol to the sheltered domesticity of Salamanca within the enclosure of the tram, the passengers dwell complacently on the glorious weather and the prospect of an equally fine lunch, their daydreams unhindered by noise and discomfort from the street. The impoverished woman seems to remain unnoticed by all except the narrator until she is unable to pay the full fare demanded by the conductor. When she cries out that her husband has abandoned her, they quickly offer financial aid, eager to bestow their charity on this example of urban destitution and misery suddenly thrust before them. Surprised and rather offended that the woman seems indifferent to their kindness and shows no gratitude, they then attempt to forget her, before hurriedly disembarking at the Calle de Goya. The narrator remains curious, however, and attempting to elicit a reaction from the woman, proceeds with pompous benevolence to advise her not to give in to her unhappiness. The woman then holds the child up in tired irritation so the narrator can see him. 'The son of the abandoned woman', the narrator realises in shock, 'was blind' [El hijo de la abandonada era ciego].[20] Illustrating the juxtapositions that take place within the city more widely, the story forces the bourgeoisie into recognition of both the enormities of social difference and their generally complacent lack of concern. The tram connects the abjection of the underside of the capital with even the relatively removed area of the Barrio de Salamanca, carrying the reality of urban poverty along its tracks, into the homes and onto the laden dining tables of the more fortunate.

The most influential Spanish woman writer of the nineteenth century, an ardent feminist campaigner and key exponent of Spanish naturalism, Pardo Bazán wrote widely on contemporary social concerns, typically focused on the gendered power dynamics of Spanish society. In another short story, 'Castaways', for example, an impoverished widow and her two daughters have arrived in Madrid in a vain search for respectable domestic employment. When a family friend finally offers the elder daughter employment in a tavern, however, both she and her mother refuse in horror. The story again takes place in spring, this time in the dusk of evening, and begins as mother and daughter are stopped by a flower-girl offering roses:

> The amethyst-tinged strawberry tones of twilight envelop the monumental views in a transparent mist flushed with ardor. Ends of tree-lined boulevards adorned with their garlands of green grow gray in the dusk. Flowering acacias overflow with fragrance, suggesting languid dreams, delicious illusions. . . . Carriages pass by . . . The women who occupy them seem more beautiful, tranquil, and relaxed, their features now blurred in the half-light, now accentuated by the glowing circle of a streetlamp or elegant boutique. [21]

Unable to pay the rent on their meagre boarding house, or even afford bread for the younger daughter, the women can only gaze wretchedly at both the natural and enhanced beauty that surrounds them. Having pawned everything of value, they are finally forced to seek out the tavern position, the daughter a victim of her lack of practical education and her father's financial incompetence. Like the woman on the tram, who only briefly disturbs the tranquility of the wealthy Salamanca, and like Galdós's Isidora Rufete, who dares to presume to the palaces of the aristocracy, the 'castaways' are illegitimate presences in the glorious avenues of the Restoration city. Eventually, Pardo Bazán implies, these 'shipwrecked women, adrift in the sea of Madrid', will also disappear altogether from the surface of the city.[22]

If the urban poor of late nineteenth-century Madrid were generally dismissed as out of sight by the Restoration regime, there was one notable space in which they were made spectacularly present. Stallybrass and White argue that in the subjective desires of the bourgeoisie, the 'low domains, apparently expelled as "Other", return as the object of nostalgia, longing and fascination'.[23] Ignoring the disturbing terrain of the outerlying slums and emphasising instead the plebeian culture of the traditional working-class *barrios* of 'old' Madrid, popular theatre at once articulated and reconstituted the bourgeois 'other' into an idealised and non-threatening object of folklore and entertainment. In their uncritical transformation from street to stage, the 'common people' became the symbolic heart of Mdrilenan identity.

From Street to Stage

The theatre, in all its forms, was perhaps the pastime par excellence of bourgeois Madrid, which recognised its potential as a social organ for the consolidation of status, affirmation of cultural taste and parade of wealth. An extraordinary number of new theatres opened across the city during the second half of the nineteenth century, including the Teatro Real (1850), Zarzuela (1856), Novedades (1857), Príncipe Alfonso (1861), Eslava (1870), Alhambra (1870), Apolo (1873), Lara (1874), Comedia (1875), Circo Price (1880), de la Princesa (1885) and Cómico (1896), evolving a new and luxurious style of theatrical architecture. Their grand design typically emphasised the role of the theatre as a performative space both on and off the stage. Behind elegant, neoclassical facades, foyers and promenades provided a rendezvous for high and bourgeois society, in which simply being part of the crowd was as, if not more, important than the events on the stage itself. The Teatro Zarzuela, for example, perhaps the model of the new architectural style, boasted a carriage entrance and grand terrace, a vestibule flanked by imposing stairways, and an enormous, horseshoe shaped auditorium. As Vicente Morant describes, the staircases, foyers, salons, balconies and galleries of the theatres, 'came to represent the highest realisation of the triumphant bourgeoisie's outlook on life' [venían a suponer la más alta consecución del modo de entender la vida por la sociedad burguesa triunfante].[24] Yet they were also spaces of mingling and encounter between bourgeois society, the middle and lower classes in the higher galleries, and more marginal urban figures equally drawn to the theatre's function as a site of self-display.

While the regular fare of Italian opera at the Teatro Real drew aristocratic and high society, however, the bourgeois public of the new democracy possessed a distinct aesthetic preference for 'one-act works, short, light and cheerful, almost picturesque, which caricature daily life, aspiring to nothing more than to distract and entertain' [prefiere obras en un acto, breves, ligeras, de carácter alegre, casi pintoresco, que caricaturizaran la vida cotidiana, sin aspirar a otra cosa que distraer y divertir].[25] Tastes were changing, and the broad urban populace demanded less exclusive, cheaper, and more comic or spectacular diversions. Moreover, if productions were shorter they not only required less time and sustained concentration on the part of audiences, but could also be performed several times over an afternoon and evening and thus offered at cheaper ticket prices. The comic entertainments offered by café-concert halls and variety theatres, for example, cost a modest price of one or two reales in the 1870s, in comparison to an average of five pesetas for a seat at the more elite Teatro Real, Teatro Español or the Teatro Circo. Light operetta and musical variety genres were common throughout Europe from the last decades of the nineteenth century, distinctly modern and urban phenomena that catered to a contemporary audience craving brief, stimulating and cheap entertainment. In Madrid, performances typically took the idiosyncratic form of the *género chico*, a one-act musical version of the eighteenth-century comic tradition of the *sainete*, based on caricatures of traditional and working-class urban life.[26] 'Theatre by the hour' (*teatro por horas*), as it became known, quickly gained mass popularity, as enthusiastically embraced by the urban elite as it was by the lower middle classes for whom it largely originated, dominating commercial theatre programmes for over half a century.

In 1890 ten of the city's theatres were dedicated almost entirely to *teatro por horas*, including the Eslava, Zarzuela, Novedades and, above all, the Teatro Apolo on the Calle de Alcalá (Fig. 4). With a capacity of 2,400, the Apolo was the largest theatre after the Teatro Real. Drawing a predominantly bourgeois and aristocratic audience, it premiered productions by the foremost writers and librettists of the time, including *La verbena de la Paloma* (1894) written by Ricardo de la Vega with music by Tomás Bretón, *Agua, azucarillos y aguardiente* (1897) by Ramos Carrión with Joaquín Valvede and Federico Chueca, and *La revoltosa* (1898) by Antonio López Silva with Carlos Fernández Shaw and Ruperto Chapí.[27] Known as the 'cathedral' of the *género chico*, it showed four performances an evening, its tremendously successful late-night show, the 'cuarta', commencing in the early hours of the morning and attended as a ritual by fashionable society. Generally less interested in the work being performed on stage, however, than in the spectacle of Madrid society enacted in front of it, the audience of the 'cuarta' visited the theatre to enjoy its own image, 'the pleasure of watching the whole of Madrid watching

Figure 4 Inauguration of the Apolo Theatre (1873), Museo Municipal de Madrid

itself' [el placer de ver a todo Madrid viéndose].[28] The auditorium of the Teatro Apolo was surrounded by a huge promenade, offering an ideal vantage point for both observation and display, as well as a notorious haunt for prostitutes. Quintessential space of the Madrilenian *belle époque*, the 'cuarta de Apolo' was the looking glass in which Restoration and Regency society paraded before its own admiring gaze.

The *género chico* combined the universal appeal of comic and sensational theatre with a distinctively local thematic and idiomatic focus, and the colour and gaiety of the traditional city was its principal and favourite leitmotif. Habitually walking the streets in quasi-ethnographic observation, the *saineteros* claimed to give a true representation of the social reality and linguistic vernacular of the traditionally working-class *barrios*. The transformation of the life and language of the streets into stage action and dialogue, however, involved a significant degree of reinvention. The limited duration of the *teatro por horas* required succinct productions which necessarily condensed narrative and characterisation. Translating the oral nature of rich slang and local accent for a printable and understandable script, moreover, was difficult, demanding the creation of phonetic words and expressions. Writers thus inevitably resorted to the use of distinctive social types, symbolic costume and appearance, and to linguistic quirks and flourishes that could be played to greatest comic effect. Lyrical comedies by dramatists such as de la Vega, López Silva and Carlos Arniches presented amusing sketches of a *costumbrismo* Madrid, their common setting the streets, taverns, market places and fiestas of the *barrios bajos*, and their characters the traders, artisans, servants, wandering sellers, night watchmen and other stereotypes that supposedly frequented them. Young men are swaggering yet honourable, young women witty and flirtatious, villains mild, and all woes satisfactorily resolved. 'One of the most distinctive characteristics of the *género chico*', describes Nancy Membrez, 'is the symbiosis of the street and the theatre, an association of culture, music and language' [Una de las características más sobresalientes del género chico es la simbiosis de la calle y el teatro, una relación cultural, musical y lingüística].[29] The *género chico* dealt in the *sound* of Madrid; the cacophony of its streets, the hum of talk, the rhythm and timbre of speech. Music and performative utterance are its mediums for thinking the city, in which the rhythms, acts and games of speech became popular symphonies and choreographies of the particular space of lower working-class Madrid. Just as the magic lantern presented Ramón Mesonero Romanos with a 'view' of the Calle de Alcalá from the Plaza de la Cebada, so the *género chico* enabled the audience of the Apolo to 'hear' the sounds of the *barrios bajos*.

The *género chico* did more than simply represent the city, whether realistically or idealistically, in a work of theatre. Most influentially, it sustained the nostalgic image of pre-industrial Madrid, even while poking satirical fun at it, creating and celebrating the myth of popular urban life enshrined as the archetypal, authentic expression of Madrilenian identity, *lo castizo*. The gist of the term *lo castizo*, however, at least according to ethnographer and writer Julio Caro Baroja, Pío Baroja's nephew, 'is not that which is pure, genuine or ancient. It is more that which best defines or is most significant of the popular at any one time' [no es lo puro o lo genuino ni lo antiguo. Es más bien lo determinativo, lo más significativo, dentro de un ámbito popular en un momento].[30] The *género chico's* theatrical expression of *castizo* Madrid drew strongly on nostalgic notions of the city's eighteenth-century populace, portrayed in the works of Goya and the *sainetes* of Ramón de la Cruz. The urban milieu of this society, and thus the emblematic space of *lo castizo*, were the old working-class *barrios* of Lavapiés, the Rastro and Embajadores, lying within the city's original walls. Largely unaffected by either disentailment or the later urban improvement plans of the nineteenth century, this delimited area between the Plaza Mayor and Puerta de Toledo was for modern eyes a spatial monument to the culture of a past age. Amidst a theatrical canvas of this familiar setting, the *chulos* and *chulas* of the contemporary plays, with their vivacity, sharp wit and streetwise attitude, are merely updated versions of Goya's smartly elegant *majos* and *majas*. Moreover, the folkloric as much as religious celebrations of the fiesta of San Isidro, and the summer *verbenas* or street fairs of the *barrios*, again common features of the city landscape in the *género chico*, offer at once expressions of and homages to *lo castizo*.[31]

That the *género chico's* greatest popularity coincided with the turn of the century and a period of turbulent social and technological change, is unsurprising. Its favourable and uncomplicated image of both nation and capital, offered a reassuring respite from fears about the technological change and social conflicts brought about by modernisation. Portraying a 'common' Madrid significantly different from the indigence of the slums observed by Baroja, writers and librettists had no intention of drawing the attention of their audience to the social problems of unemployment, poverty, unsanitary conditions, infant mortality, prostitution, suicide and crime that plagued the turn-of-the-century city. The festivities of Madrilenian folklore were far more reassuring for a society in which popular anxieties over the stability of the bourgeoisie, and the social and political degeneration of the nation as a whole, were rife. By stereotyping and light-heartedly ridiculing the lower classes, the *género chico* both differentiated them from its bourgeois and upwardly mobile petit-bourgeois audiences, and discharged any sense of revolutionary threat. Simultaneously, although somewhat paradoxically, it idealises a traditional, popular way of life that stood at the mythic heart of Madrilenian identity. For if traditional festivity was 'simply one of the many casualties in the movement towards an urban, industrial society' across bourgeois Europe, through its '*displacements* into bourgeois discourses', gained a new symbolic prevalence.[32] Geographically demarcated within the area and landmarks of old Madrid, the *castizo* festivals and *verbenas* of the *barrios*, were at once removed from the modern bourgeois city, yet also unproblematically assimilable as part of its cultural heritage.

Despite the debacle of the colonial war of 1898, Arniches, for example, continued to observe the city with a satirical but loyal and enthusiastic eye, very different to the pessimism and repulsion with which it was viewed by his contemporary regenerationists. In his *El santo de Isidra* and *La fiesta de San Antón*, both premiered in 1898, the life of the *barrios bajos* remains vibrantly and colourfully unaffected by contemporary disillusionment and unrest. The former is set during the fiesta of Madrid's patron saint San Isidro, traditionally celebrated by a lively picnic at the Pradera de San Isidro, a meadow to the south-west of the city. The romantic and predictable plot, a rivalry between a shy and gentle baker and thuggish bully for the affections of the lively heroine, is slight and little more than a pretext for the animated depiction of the popular fiesta. The stage sets, stereotypical characters and depictions of local colour, however, are revealing of the *género chico*'s formulaic presentation of *castizo* Madrid. The play opens amidst preparations for the festivities in a small square in the emblematic heart of the old city, adjacent to the Calle de Toledo and in view of the Plaza de Cebada. Far from a place of poverty and degradation, this is an ebullient centre of local commerce, flanked on the left by a grocer's shop, and on the right, its balcony hung with flowers, a tavern.[33] The pradera of the latter scenes is a space of 'extraordinary animation' [Animación extraordinaria], evoking 'the tumultuous, deafening sounds of the fair, barrel organs, street musicians, drum-rolls, voices, the shouts of vendors, the clamour of the people, etc.' [mezclados los estrepitosos ruidos de la fiesta, organillos, murgas, redobles de tambor, voces, gritos de vendedores, algaraza de la gente, etcétera], as revellers dance, blow whistles and rush to the carrousels and swings.[34] Arniches offered his audience an escape from the disorientations of the modern, cheerfully assuring them of the stable geniality of their city – and they adored him for it.

The people of the traditional *barrios* seem to have been willing participants in this mythification, performing the image presented of them on the stage, and even offering themselves or their acquaintances as representative subjects. P. Lozano Guirao notes that with the enormous success of *La verbena de la Paloma*, for example, Ricardo de la Vega 'spread and implanted customs that in time became rooted in the purest essence of popular culture' [Difundió e implantó costumbres que con el tiempo arraigaron en la más pura esencia de lo popular], as well as returning the 'manton de Manila', the Chinese silk shawl that Galdós had shown declining in favour with the mid-nineteenth-century bourgeoisie of *Fortunata y Jacinta*, to the height of fashion.[35] When young women rushed to adopt the look of Susana and Casta, the female protagonists of the play, however, as they would again in response to the popular film versions of 1921 and 1935, they were not falsifying a 'genuine' *castizo* identity through the uncritical adoption of the images of modern mass entertainment. The trademark speech, dress and postures brought into cultural circulation by the theatre, resonated with modern as well as traditional meaning, and as such could be employed for the knowing performance of a current vogue.

Arniches, speaking in an interview in 1917, described, 'I enter any bar . . . At first my presence is considered strange. Later, the same barmen assist me in my objectives. "Don Carlos – they say to me – today you are going to meet a typical fellow"' [entro en alguna taberna . . . Al principio, mi presencia extraña. Después, los mismos taberneros favorecen mis propósitos. "Don Carlos – me dicen – hoy va a conocer usted un tipo"].[36] Acknowledging this mutual mimicry between reality and fiction, López Silva likewise admitted that 'while I was endeavouring to copy the language of ordinary people, polite society was copying the idioms and sayings of my plays and verse dialogues' [al mismo tiempo que yo copiaba el lenguaje del pueblo, las buenas gentes copiaban los modismos y decires de mi teatro y de mis diálagos en verso].[37] Of course the street and stage were not entirely blurred spaces. As Vicente Blasco Ibáñez somewhat drily commented, 'they are not the same. López Silva's characters speak in verse, and in the slums of Madrid, as in the rest of the world, people speak in prose, . . . if the common people of Madrid were to speak exactly like the characters of López Silva, the poet would have absolutely no reason to be or exist' [no son iguales. Los personajes de López Silva hablan en verso, y en los barrios bajos de Madrid, como en el resto del mundo, la gente es prosaica, . . . si la gente menuda de los Madriles hablase exactamente como los personajes de López Silva, no tendría el poeta ninguna razón de ser y existir].[38] Yet the *género chico* undoubtedly influenced the collective consciousness of Madrid, authenticating a social, cultural and linguistic urban identity that it was itself instrumental in creating. Indeed, through the common acceptance of the *castizo* Madrid that it promoted, popular theatre branded the space and everyday life of the *barrios* into a commodity. In the notion of *lo castizo* we find an archetype of the cultural configuration of urban identity, in which stage and street interconnect in the production, circulation and reproduction of a specific metropolitan personality and temperament.

One of the most successful lyrical comedies of the Restoration period, *La Gran Vía*, which opened at the Teatro Felipe in the Jardines del Buen Retiro in July 1886, interestingly considers the city in terms of its future built form as much as its traditional customs. Written by Felipe Pérez y González and set to a suite of popular dances by Chueca and Valverde, it takes the form of a *Revista*, a sub-genre of the *género chico* characterised by its current and topical focus on the politics, fashions and events of the Madrid scene.[39] Evoking a recognisable map of late nineteenth-century Madrid, the action follows a protagonist and his allegorical companion, Caballero de Gracia (the name of a central street between the Calle de

Alcalá and the Calle de Montera), as they walk through the various *barrios* and areas of the city prior to the inauguration of a new, modern boulevard; from the calles and plazas of its traditional centre, to the indigent outskirts of Injurias, Pacífico and Prósperidad, the Puerta del Sol and the pleasure ground of the Campos Elíseos. Joking and arguing about the new avenue, the performers take on the personas of these well-known Madrid streets and sites, their varying status within the urban map denoted by the style of the musical score, from the 'polka of the streets', to the 'waltz of the Caballero de Gracia'.

Typically light-hearted entertainment, and with little semblance of plot, *La Gran Vía* yet also offers an allegorical social commentary on a specific issue within the urban politics of contemporary Madrid; the plan for a monumental, east–west artery running north of the Puerta del Sol from the Plaza de San Marcial to the Calle de Alcalá, presented earlier in the year by architect Carlos Velasco. Extensively remodelling the existing urban layout, the project required the complicated expropriation of large amounts of land and was quickly abandoned. Nevertheless, the prospect of a glorious boulevard or *gran vía* that would proclaim Madrid as a modern metropolis, had become a cherished fancy of the collective urban imagination. Projecting this onto the stage, programme covers and set design depicted the avenue as a long, straight, Parisian-style boulevard, lined with street lamps and overlooked by tall, elegant buildings. Describing the closing scene González writes:

> the theatre represents a town square which opens onto an immense, wide avenue, magnificent in every way, lined by sumptuous facades. . . . In the centre of the square stands a monument, crowned by a statue of Liberty carrying the Spanish flag in her right hand. The four corners of the pedestal are decorated with other figures, representing Science, Justice, Work and Virtue. All the buildings are adorned and illuminated as if for a great fair.
>
> [el teatro representa una plaza de la que parte una vía inmensa, anchurosa y por todos conceptos magnífica, formada por edificios suntuosos. . . . En el centro de la plaza se eleva un monumento al que sirve de remate la estatua de Libertad, que tiene en la mano derecha la bandera española. En los cuatro ángulos del pedestal hay otros tantas figuras que representan la Ciencia, la Justicia, el Trabajo y la Virtud. Todos los edificios estaran colgados y iluminados como en día de grande fiesta].[40]

Anticipating a future Madrid, at the same time as celebrating the city of the present and evoking nostalgia for the familiar spaces of that soon to disappear, *La Gran Vía* epitomised the paradoxically *castizo and* modernising city of the turn of the century. Between the imaginary creation of Madrid's new boulevard on stage in 1886, and the realisation in asphalt of its first section by 1917, the city would finally take on the appearance of a modern metropolis. 'I remember returning to Madrid in the summer in which *La Gran Vía* opened', Baroja wrote, 'for many madrileñians of the time, this epoch must have been a landmark of their existence' [Recuerdo haber vuelto a Madrid en el verano en que se estrenó *La Gran Vía*. Para muchos madrileños del tiempo, esta época debió de ser un hito de su existencia].[41] Julio Caro Baroja recalls that despite laughing at Arniches' humour and admiring Chueca's melodies, his uncle in general disliked the romantic 'madrileñismo' of the *género chico*.[42] It is ironic that Baroja's first conception of Madrid was dominated by the innocuous popular theatre that his own writing of the city would diametrically oppose. It would be a decade before new legislation would allow reconsideration of the Velasco project, and two before the plans for a similar avenue by architects José López Sallaberry and Francisco Andrés Octavio were approved. Meanwhile, the public still flocked to see their new 'gran vía'; only as it was recreated in the theatre rather than the street.

–5–

Cosmopolitan Lights

Modern technology resulted in a fundamental transformation of the temporality and spatiality of urban life. The electrification of public lighting and trams, along with the development of the metro, the telegraph, the elevator and the cinema, reconfigured the physical form, social culture and subjective experience of the city. As electricity illuminated Madrid by night, the first skyscrapers pierced its skyline, and the metropolitan railway transported passengers through its subterranean depths, practices and perceptions of urban space were profoundly altered, the city becoming at once newly ordered and newly mysterious. For if electricity, epitomising progress and scientific technology, illuminated, rationalised and standardised the urban landscape, it was also a strangely invisible phenomenon, an ether with the power to annihilate time and distance, made manifest through the spaces and machines of the city.

Electrifying Space

Electric light was first used publicly in Madrid in celebration of the wedding of Alfonso XII in 1878, when the streets and buildings of the Puerta del Sol were illuminated with electric lamps, providing a spectacular stage for the performance of modern monarchical splendour. The general electrification of the city began five years later with the inauguration of the Sociedad Matritense de Electricidad, created by the city council to provide lighting in the Ministry of War. The network covered a broad central area, including the Puerta del Sol, its surrounding streets, and the Parque del Retiro, illuminating previously familiar public spaces with an unusual brilliance. As David Nye argues, it is important not to underestimate the initial impact of electrification on the urban populations of the late nineteenth century, to whom newly electrified cities would have seemed almost supernatural spaces, illuminated with a strange light 'at once mild and intense, smokeless, fireless, steady, seemingly inexhaustible'.[1] On the one hand regulating and disciplining city space, electric light was also enabling, opening up the previously illicit night world to the respectable public and encouraging a new phenomenon of urban night-life. In the Puerta del Sol, for example, where shops often traded until late in the evening, many of the cafés and bun-shops would remain open throughout the night, Baroja recalling that '[t]his gave the city an air of turbulence and mystery, and of joy. Many rich and middle-class people were night-owls' [Esto daba al pueblo un aire de turbulencia y de misterio, y de alegría. Mucha gente rica y de la clase media era noctámbula].[2] With the recognition of the functional possibilities and commercial benefits of the new fuel, competing private companies quickly developed, providing electricity across the city by the end of the century, but domestic consumption predominantly remained restricted to the wealthier *barrios* of the northern suburbs. Juxtaposed with the shimmering public spaces of the street, shop, café, restaurant and theatre, the gloom of the private interior was by comparison made all the darker. Electrical technology thus brought with it an 'electrical' imagination and sensibility, the new infrastructure of the city influencing a new mode of observing it, in which 'landscape was no longer experienced intensively, but evanescently, impressionistically'.[3] Ramón Gómez de la Serna, for example, eulogised electrification for its transformation of the city into a surreal and transcendent space: 'Now, on leaving the Metro and entering the Puerta del Sol, one is even more dazzled. It is as if we emerge into another world' [Ahora, cuando se sale del Metro y se aparece en la Puerta del Sol, su deslumbramiento es mucho mayor. Parece que salimos a otro mundo] (*HPS*, 118).

Transforming the appearance of the city, electricity also altered the way in which its spaces were traversed. The tram network was fully electrified by 1902, smooth-running, metallic tramlines replacing the chaos and organic waste of horse power. The tram had at once a centrifugal and centripetal effect on the growth and functional zoning of the city, encouraging relocation out to the suburbs as a direct result of its facilitating rapid access back in. The increasing traffic from the urban periphery, however, descended on the chaotic street network of an archaic city centre. In the dense traffic hub of the Puerta del Sol, trams, cars and taxis competed for space with horse-drawn carriages, wandering sellers and pedestrians, to hazardous effect. The writer Azorín, for example, commenting in 1902, presents an apocalyptic vision of the city of modernity:

There is a barbarity more horrific than that of ancient times: modern industrialism, the desire for profit, collective exploitation in rail and banking companies, blind subjection, in the street, in the café, in the theatre, to the all-powerful market. Trains that collide and derail, electric trams, early trams that knock down and deafen with the ringing of their bells and their roaring, electric wires that fall and kill on the spot, cars crossing in all directions.
[Hay una barbarie más hórrida que la barbarie antigua: el industrialismo moderno, el afán de lucro, la explotación colectiva en empresas ferroviarias y bancarias, el sujetamiento insensible, en la calle, en el café, en el teatro, al mercador prepotente. Trenes que chocan y descarrilan, tranvías eléctricos, prematuros tranvías que atropellan y ensordecen con sus campanilleos y rugidos, hilos eléctricos que caen y súbitamente matan, coches que cruzan en todas las direcciones].[4]

Azorín's Madrid is fraught with risk, from the social and psychological exploitation and control of the modern money society, to the immediate physical danger
of the street, and in which fatality might dramatically strike at any moment.

Two decades later, the population density of the city centre, the congestion of
the Puerta del Sol, and the serious measures required to aid the circulation of
commuter traffic into and across the city, had become a widely recognised issue.
The metropolitan railway system was inaugurated in 1919, its first line running
between Cuatro Caminos and the Puerta del Sol, and went some way to relieving
the pressure on the roads leading into the centre. By 1925 it had extended to
the *barrio* of Puente de Vallecas, forming an underground transport channel
that linked the working-class residential areas of the north and south-east with
the city centre. Above ground, however, the streets remained hazardously chaotic.
'Madrid is a city that is permanently congested' [Madrid es una población perpet-
uamente congestionada], complained a journalist in the newspaper *ABC* in 1920,
reporting:

> Yesterday's incident is almost a daily occurrence. On one of the central roads of Madrid
> traffic was at a standstill for a long period. Trams, buses, cars of every type, carts and
> crowds of pedestrians had converged there. The very existence of the town and court
> collapsed.
> [El incidente que occurrió ayer se repite casi todos las días. En una de las vías centrales
> de Madrid quedó interrumpida la circulación durante largo rato. Se habían reunido allí
> tranvías, autos, coches de diversas categorías, carros y multitud de gente de a pie. La villa
> y corte sufrió un colapso en su existencia][5]

The designation of the city as 'town and court' perhaps reveals the commentator's
own opinions on the reason for such regular annoyances. Continuing to berate the
conditions of the city centre in irate tone, for example, he argues:

> The Madrilenian is a city-dweller who cannot leave his house. If he does go out, he must
> brave the dangers of isolation. The tram that does not appear, the horse-drawn carriage
> that is nowhere to be found, the public bus that is virtually non-existent, the street
> blocked by a build up of carriages and pedestrians.
> [El madrileño es un ciudadano que no puede salir de su casa. Si sale, ha de sufrir los
> peligros de la incomunicación. El tranvía que no llega, el simón que no se encuentra, el
> auto de servicio público que prácticamente no existe, la calle que se obtura por la
> acumulación de carruajes y de transeuntes]

The description of the lack of transport in a city congested by all types of traffic,
although paradoxical, nevertheless evokes the frustratingly underdeveloped
infrastructure of the city centre. The two most dramatic proposals for urban reform
were strikingly opposed in both design and intention. The first was the ultimately

anti-urban solution of a self-contained, low-rise satellite city, economically independent from the traditional Madrid core. The other was the creation of a direct
east–west thoroughfare across the city, that would bypass the Puerta del Sol
to connect with the Calle de Alcalá and link with the north–south axis of the
Castellana at the Plaza de Cibeles – the cherished Gran Vía.

Rectilinear Cities

Conceived in the 1880s by Arturo Soria, an engineering entrepreneur who had
already worked in both the telegraph and railway industries, the 'linear city'
offered a functional and progressive response to the continued problem of demographic growth. Soria's plan, published in 1892 as 'La Ciudad Lineal', imagined
a series of decentralised, business and industrial-based urban nuclei, circumventing
Madrid and connected by an interconnecting transport corridor. The linear city
would be constructed either side of this principal avenue, between 30 and 40
metres wide and along which rail and trolley-car tracks would run above ground,
and gas and water pipes below. Offices, factories, commercial stores and municipal
buildings would line the central corridor, with private, individual housing built
parallel to it, between smaller, transverse streets. These, in turn, linked the still
largely agrarian economy of the countryside with the central arterial access route,
and finally with Madrid and other linear cities.

Soria promoted the multiple benefits of his plan in numerous articles; detailing
its efficiency for the circulation of goods and people, its healthy and pleasant
environment, its social and political order.[6] For alongside its formal practicality for
the industrial and commercial economy, the linear city was also an experiment in
ethical planning, expressing Soria's ultimately social Darwinist belief that spatial
environment shaped human attitudes and behaviour. The *dis*organization of traditional urban space, he argued, cramped, chaotic and socially segregated, resulted
in dissatisfaction, disease and crime. The solution to these problems of urban
modernity was the total reconstruction of the *form* of the city, into an ordered,
harmonious, neatly geometric space. With its intention of 'contributing to the
material and moral good of Madrid' [contribuyendo al bien material y moral
de Madrid], the Ciudad Lineal promised a rational and hygienic urban utopia,
resembling to a certain extent Ebenezer Howard's garden city concept, but based
in a belief in the value of modern transport technology.[7] It would do nothing to
counter the conditions of extreme poverty highlighted by Baroja, but it did intend
to provide an improved standard of living for skilled workers and the average-
income middle classes.

Despite Soria's claims, the linear city seemed to have no answer to the issue of
social stratification, with the largest and most expensive villas built nearest to the

main street, a middle-price range facing the intersecting streets and the cheapest furthest away.[8] Indeed this zoning of the residential area would seem to repeat the Castro plan and produce an even greater segregation than in central Madrid, where the tradition of classes being separated by the different levels of individual buildings rather than by neighbourhood produced, certainly according to Galdós, a blurring of social status. Yet the residential land of the linear city was divided by its economic value in relation to the principal avenue, not by the whims of urban planning, and Soria's intention was to provide each man with the possibility of owning his own property, thus raising quality of living. Of course the linear city was always primarily intended to cater for the business class of modernity, the entrepreneurs, industrialists, financiers and professionals of the bourgeois middle class who relied on social stability for economic profit. Isolated private housing for all would promote the status quo by discouraging collective discord amongst the working classes through the development of a greater culture of individuality in everyday life. A moderate liberal whose values coupled modernisation with conservatism, he had learned the lessons of Haussmann well. The arterial thoroughfare and connecting streets of the linear city could facilitate the rapid movement of the military as much as of people and freight.

In 1894 Soria formed the Compañía Madrileño de Urbanización and set about the promotion of the linear city, the acquisition of land and the securing of political and financial backing. Construction began the same year, and by 1900 the transport corridor, although reduced to only a tramline, linked the new Ciudad Lineal with central Madrid. In 1911 over seven hundred properties had been completed, and the suburb had a population of 4,000. The practical problems with Soria's ideal were soon evident, notably the impossibility of property-ownership for all but the upper echelons of the Madrid working class. When the average wage of a labourer with a family was less than 100 pesetas per month, few could afford even the relatively reasonable price of 3,600 pesetas for the smallest, four-room dwellings. Focusing solely on the physical structures of urban space as the solution to the problems of modernity, Soria ignored the fact that urban poverty and civil unrest were as much the result of the social and economic structures of society that the linear city upheld. Financial depression and political instability after the First World War checked progress, however, and with Soria's death in 1920 the project was eventually suspended.

Concurrent with Soria's development of his utopian 'linear city' outside Madrid, the long-awaited Gran Vía was finally being constructed at its centre. Revising Velasco's original blueprint, the Salaberry and Octavio scheme for the Gran Vía divided the avenue into three sections: the first running from the fork of the Calle Alcalá and the Caballero de Gracia to the Red de San Luis, where it would intersect with the metro-line to and from the Puerta del Sol, the second continuing from the Red to the Plaza de Callao, and the third from Callao to the new western access route of the Plaza de España and Calle de la Princesa. Construction started in 1910 at a cost of twenty-nine million pesetas. Coinciding with the economic boom period and architectural expansiveness of the First World War, the Gran Vía quickly became most significant not so much as a functional transport corridor, than as the ultimate manifestation of Madrid's urge to architectural and cultural modernity. Business investment made the avenue a new urban hub in its own right, a spatial demonstration of the social ascendancy of money, modern commerce and mass culture. Architect Secundino Zuazo, for example, described it as the equivalent of the financial 'City' of other modern metropoli, a convergence of economic authority in the form of the headquarters and offices of banking and telecommunication institutions, as well as cosmopolitan leisure spaces, department stores, hotels and luxury apartments.[9]

Following the example of Haussmann in Paris, the trajectory of Madrid's central modern avenue required the categorical demolition of a large area of slum housing. A single boulevard, the Gran Vía was a work of urban reform on a much smaller scale than Haussman's Paris, but its construction nevertheless significantly transformed both the built form and the social and cultural zoning of the city. The area north of the Puerta del Sol that the new avenue was to bisect was old and impoverished, the majority of streets narrow and unhygienic, its houses tiny and with little ventilation. Fifty streets were altered in the scheme, and fourteen destroyed altogether, resulting in what for contemporary commentators was perhaps the city council's most decisive action against Madrid's slum conditions. Such utopian urban 'sanitation', however, merely eliminated the visibility of urban poverty by displacing and abjecting it to the remote periphery. A single modern avenue, slashing its way through a part of the city that had remained almost unchanged since the sixteenth century, the heights of the Gran Vía presented a symbolic and architectural façade of Western modernity, hiding not only the shabby and impoverished areas that lay directly to its north and south, but also the entrenched political and social ideology of the Spanish capital. With no attempt made to create a transitional zone between the new avenue and the older city that it bisected, it stood in sharp juxtaposition with the narrow, archaic streets and impoverished life that lay on its immediate borders.

The luxury buildings of the first stage of the Gran Vía emulated the decorative classicism of the Parisian *belle époque*, epitomised for example by the Edificio Metrópolis, designed for the insurance company of La Unión y Fénix by French architects Jules and Raymond Février. By the construction of the central section, however, urban design had turned to the new architectural influence of New York, and the street began to assume the towering height that would distinguish it so dramatically from the rest of the city. The skyscraper was embraced by urban planners as the architectural icon of twentieth-century urban modernity, described enthusiastically by Zuazo, for example, as 'close to one of the great technical inventions of the present' [la que más se asemeja a las grandes creaciones técnicas del presente]. The second section of the Gran Vía, at thirty-five metres wide much broader than the first, was lined with buildings that, while not approaching the proportions of American skyscrapers, dominated the city skyline; the department store of Almacenes Madrid-París (Teodoro Anasagasti, 1922), the Palacio de la Prensa (Muguruza, 1928), housing the offices of the Madrid Press Association, hotels such as the Atlántico (Joaquín Saldaña, 1920) and the Alfonso XII (Antonio Palacios, 1925), and La Telefónica (Lewis Weeks and Ignacio Cárdenas, 1929), the headquarters of the American telecommunication company ITT. Their soaring edifices are clearly visible in aerial photographs from the first half of the twentieth century, rising in linear relief from the rest of the city (Fig. 5).

Figure 5 *Vista aérea de la Gran Vía* (1930), Archivo General de la Administración, Madrid

The beacon of the newly cosmopolitan Madrid, however, standing at the aperture of the final section, was the Edificio Carrión (Luis Martínez Feduchi and Vicente Eced y Eced, 1933), a multi-use building that included all the composite elements of modern urbanity: a hotel, cinema, bars and restaurants, offices, studios, and luxury flats for rent. The electric elevator, so crucial to the building of the skyscraper, nullified the social stratification or segregation of traditional urban living space in the city. In contrast to both the apartment buildings of the old city, where owners or wealthy tenants occupied the lower floors, letting the higher levels and attic spaces to the lower classes, and the bourgeois mansions of the suburban Salamanca, the new buildings of the Gran Vía provided modern opulent accommodation in the centre of the city. Land was at a premium but, with the access provided by the elevator, height gained financial value and elite status. The elegant flats of the Edificio Metrópolis, and the multi-use buildings of the Palacio de la Prensa and the Carrión, for example, were all financed by companies and entrepreneurs recognising the investment potential of real estate. The epitome of this combination of work, leisure and residential space, the Carrión offered a self-contained, vertical city in its own right, a luxury world set apart from the contested space of the street below. Yet long a theatrical space in the truest sense, in its built reality the Gran Vía resembled Walter Benjamin's first impressions of the Parisian boulevard; a space 'not to be lived in, but to pass between – the way one passes through the wings in a theater'.[10]

The construction of the Gran Vía undoubtedly had an apocalyptic effect on the map of the city centre. The artist and writer José Gutiérrez Solana, in *Madrid callejero* (1923), a series of urban tableaux written with *castizo* sentiment but that in an inversion of *costumbrismo* focus on the destruction of traditional spaces and customs, depicts the Gran Vía as entirely alien to the city. Born in 1886, his memories of the city's dream of a 'great avenue' were of the cheerful humming of his nanny as a child in arms, or of the cook as she made hot chocolate (*MC*, 43). The contemporary boulevard, however, is a hideous distortion of its aborted fantasy. Contrasting the statue of Liberty that had stood as a backdrop to the theatrical avenue of the zarzuela, with the plight of 'the former residents of these old streets, forced to pack up their belongings and move on, by force of suffering and looting' [los antiguos vecinos de estas viejas calles, que han tenido que irse con las trastos a otra parte, a fuerza de sufrimientos y expoliaciones] (*MC*, 44), he critiques the 'uselessness' [inutilidad] (*MC*, 45) of its ostentatious luxury:

> The old streets have been replaced by this new network, full of pompous modern buildings, all extremely white, in Catalan in style, without a shred of skill or character; . . . The shops are as stylistically pretentious as the houses: a great profusion of light, in which wax mannequins display garish, pretentious clothes for bourgeois tastes; . . . In others luxurious automobiles are exhibited, the ideal of the new rich

[A las antiguas calles ha sucedio esta nueva red, llena de edificios a la moderna, petulantes, todos muy blancos, estilo catalán, y en los que no se ve ni por asomo un poco de arte y personalidad; . . . Las tiendas son del mismo estilo pretencioso que las casas: gran derroche de luz, en que se muestran, sobre maniquís de cera, ropas de bazar, pretenciosas y de gusto burgués; . . . En otros se exhiben los automóviles lujosos, ideal de los nuevos ricos]. (*MC*, 44)

From a space of *castizo* entertainment framed by the *género chico*, the Gran Vía has become in its built form a space of mass-culture, Solana gloomily offering an inventory of its frivolous goods and ambience: 'gramophones, mechanical music, mixed with photographs and autographs of more or less long-haired movie stars; . . . restaurants that are crowded in the evenings, and where the people dance to negro music' [gramófonos, música mecánica, alternando con fotografías y autógrafos de divos más o menos melenudos; . . . los restaurantes, muy frecuentados por las tardes y en los que se baila con música de negro] (*MC*, 55). For Solana the Gran Vía represents a mechanised, artificial culture that is, most importantly, extremely un-Madrilenian. Like his earlier negative reference to Catalan architecture, however, the allusion to 'negro' music, and the later description of people sitting on bar stools so high that they resemble monkeys, gives a distastefully racial bias to his censure.

Modernity, internationalism and Americanism were repeatedly collapsed in the rhetoric of the new boulevard, across the discourses of urban design, commercial advertising, aesthetic representation and social critique, as well as in the practices of fashionable everyday life. Edward Baker notes that Madrid's new modernity was 'unmistakably North American' [inconfundiblemente norteamericano], and that 'the second section of the Gran Vía was the setting, or rather the stage, for the new past-times and the new, unmistakably cosmopolitan habits of collective life' [Fue el segundo tramo de la Gran Vía el espacio, diríase mejor escenario, de los nuevos ocios y de las nuevas formas de vida colectiva inconfundiblemente cosmopolitas].[11] As their names indicate, bars such as Chicote's, Miami, Casablanca and Hollywood, capitalised on the contemporary fashion for all things exotic and above all American, serving cocktails and vibrating with the rhythms of Manhattan and Harlem; the 'shimmy', the 'two-step' and the 'fox-trot'.[12] What perhaps most marked the contemporary Gran Vía, however, was its dense concentration of movie theatres, which included the Callao (Luis Gutiérrez Soto, 1927) and the Palacio de la Música (Secundino Zuazo, 1928), as well as those within the buildings of Madrid-París, the Palacio de la Prensa, the Carrión and the Coliseum (Fernández Shaw, 1932). Picture palaces in the truest sense, they made the Gran Vía, Madrid's showcase of modernity and mass reproduction, seem a world of only cinemas and dreams.

The Urban Cinematograph

Madrid was introduced to the 'moving picture' in May 1895, with the exhibition of the Edison kinetoscope at the company's studio on the Carrera de San Jerónimo. The Lumière brothers' cinematograph, the apparatus that arguably pioneered the development of cinema by projecting moving images for a group audience, was first presented in Spain a year later, five months after its inauguration in Paris, in the basement of the Hotel Rusia in Madrid.[13] After two private screenings, the first for members of the aristocracy and government, and the second for the press, it opened to the general public on 15 May, the Fiesta of San Isidro. Showings took place between ten and twelve o'clock in the morning, three and seven in the afternoon, and from nine to eleven at night. Organised by a M. Promio, the Lumière representative in Madrid, several Spanish shorts were incorporated into the general programme, including two that focused on the symbolic Madrilenian sites of the Puerta de Toledo and the Puerta del Sol.

It seems appropriate, if somewhat paradoxical, that Madrid's introduction to the cosmopolitan entertainment form of the twentieth century should take place amidst the traditional fiesta of its patron saint, and even more so that it should coincide with the premiere of Chueca and Valverde's celebrated *La Gran Vía*. The promised boulevard that in 1896 was the collective dream of the bourgeois theatre-going public, would in the 1920s become Madrid's own 'cinemaland'. In the early years of the cinematograph in Spain, as elsewhere, projections typically took place in show-booths at fairs and fiestas, or in temporary projection theatres, such as those erected in the Calle de Alcalá, the Calle de Atocha and the Plaza de Antón Martín. By the end of the century regular screenings of moving pictures began to take place within variety theatres and circus. Seven theatres were registered as presenting cinematographic events in 1900, for example, including the Teatro Romea, the Salón de Actualidades, the Teatro Zarzuela and the Circo de Parish. With the construction of moving picture theatres in their own right from 1915, this figure boomed, from twenty-one in 1920 to over sixty by 1936.[14]

The initial response of the press to the spectacle of the Lumière cinematograph, typically emphasised its ability to capture the reality of everyday life. 'The illusion is perfect', stated the newspaper *El País*, 'and the effect . . . better than reality itself' [La illusion es completa y el efecto . . . es superior a la misma realidad].[15] Of the leading writers, artists and intellectuals who attended the private screening, few were immediately struck by the aesthetic potential of moving pictures as a creative art. By the 1920s, however, cinema had become a topic of intellectual debate both in specialist publications on film aesthetics, such as *La Pantalla and El Cine*, and the literary magazines of *La Revista de Occidente* and *La Gaceta Literaria*.[16] If Miguel Unamuno was still claiming that 'literature has no role to play in the cinema' [La literatura nada tiene que hacer en el cinematógrafo], other writers were embracing silent film as a modern aesthetic in its own right, influential for the form and structure of literature and art themselves.[17] Acclaimed as a radical new art, and as a potential instrument of social enlightenment, cinema perhaps above all stimulated a new form of perception. The interplay of light and shadow in film projection, the cinematic techniques of montage, simultaneity, close-up and long-shot, and the exaggerated, pantomime-like acts and slapstick comedy of silent films, for example, subverted the conventional angles, frames and rhythms of visual experience. 'It was cinema . . . that revealed for the first time, the graphic and plastic value of isolated images' [El cinema . . . es lo que hizo ver, por vez primera, el valor gráfico y plástico de los imágenes sueltas], stated Guillermo de la Torre in 1934, 'the beauty, the drama, the humour or the superreality of certain shreds of real life that we did not notice before' [la belleza, el dramatismo, el humor o la supperrealidad de ciertos jirones reales que antes no advertíamos].[18]

'The cinema speaks only to our eyes', Ramón del Valle-Inclán wrote in 1922.[19] Two years earlier, he had depicted the nocturnal underworld of an impoverished, bohemian Madrid in a play dominated by images and metaphors of vision, *Luces de Bohemia* ('Bohemian Lights', 1920). Set within a 'Madrid absurd, brilliant and hungry' [un Madrid absurdo, brillante y hambriento] (*LBo*, 85), the action takes place during the hours of one evening, amidst the fetid urban map of a turn-of-the-century city prior to the construction of the Gran Vía. Beginning at twilight, it follows the blind and destitute poet Máximo Estrella as he journeys through a series of progressively sordid city sites, in search of money that is owed to him, before his death from alcohol and hypothermia in the early hours of the following morning. Seemingly an incongruous urban *flâneur*, the sightless Estrella is nevertheless the absurd and anti-heroic vehicle through which Valle-Inclán presents a piercing critique of Western society, and Spain in particular, in the first decades of the twentieth century. As his surname Estrella ('star') suggests, he is a guide to the infinite shadows of urban life, oblivious to the blinding, manipulating artificial light of technological modernity. Precisely because he is himself already blind, Estrella is only aware of the natural darkness of the city, and its highly visual pretensions to modernity are thus meaningless to him. His journey takes him not through the new, brightly illuminated Madrid of the twentieth century, but into the depths of the old city of half-light and shadow that it has abjected, a city that he understands through the grotesque projections of his own frustrated and suffering mind.

Valle-Inclán's clear adherence to the Madrid street map of the first decade of the twentieth century, reveals that Estrella's quest takes him to the various bohemian haunts of the area on the fringe of, or destroyed by, the site of the Gran Vía, as his readers would be well aware, thus geographically bordering the new city whilst otherwise remaining far removed from its glossy modernity. From his meagre house in the centre of the old city, he visits a second-hand bookshop just north of the Puerta del Sol, a tavern in the Calle Montera, the Buñoleria Modernista (a coffee shop, probably located near the Calle Hortaleza), makes a brief detour to the Puerta del Sol when he is accidentally caught up in a political disturbance and detained in the cells of the Ministerio de la Gobernación (Home Office), before continuing to a café in the Calle Colón, and returning home via the Paseo de Recoletos. If Valle-Inclán exploits the multiple potential of the metaphors of vision, darkness, illumination and projection for the theme of *Luces de bohemia*, he also draws on the effects of cinema for the dramatisation of its location. Stage directions, for example, are written in montage, as in the portrayal of a bar on the Calle Montera, 'The tavern of Pica Lagartos: Light from oil lamps: a zinc counter: A dark hall full of tables and benches: Card players: Muffled dialogue. Máximo Estrella and Don Latino de Hispalis, shadows in the shadows of a corner' [La taberna de Pica Lagartos: Luz de acetileno: Mostrador de cinc: Zaguán oscuro con mesas y banquillos: Jugadores de mus: Borrosas diálogos. Máximo Estrella y Don Latino de Hispalis, sombras en las sombras de un rincón] (*LBo*, 102), or characterised by the optical potency of the interplay of light and shade on spaces, faces and objects, and the association of sound with visual image:

> Night. . . . Moonlight on the eaves of the houses, cutting the street in two. From time to time the asphalt resonates. . . . The echo of the patrol dies away. The door of the Buñoleria Modernista opens slightly, and a shaft of light cuts across the pavement. [Noche. . . . La luna sobre el alero de las casas, partiendo la calle por medio. De tarde en tarde, el asfalto sonoro. . . . Se extingue el eco de la patrulla. La Buñoleria Modernista entreaba su puerta, y una banda de luz parte la acera]. (*LBo*, 112)

For Valle-Inclán, the techniques of cinema suggested methods and metaphors for writing the visual force of the city, its constant succession of images in all their manifold simultaneity.

The early cinema of the fairgrounds, variety theatres and show-booths, far from the supreme art of illusory veracity that began to typify film in the 1920s, was a medium that exposed the strangeness of the mundane familiarity of the everyday, and it is perhaps this theatrical 'cinema of attractions' that best relates to Valle-Inclán's cinematic vision in *Luces de bohemia*. In 1910s and 1920s Madrid, passers-by on the Calle Álvarez Gato, an alleyway near the Puerta del Sol, could stop to look at distorted reflections of themselves in concave mirrors that stood outside a hardware store, as a plaque in the wall of the restaurant that now stands on the site commemorates. For Valle-Inclán, the grotesque images provided a succinct visual metaphor of modern life, and that of Madrid in particular. Shortly before dying, Max likens contemporary Spain to the reflections of the fairground mirrors: 'Spain is a grotesque deformation of European civilization. . . . In a concave mirror, the most beautiful images are absurd' [España es una deformación grotesca de la civilización europea. . . . Las imagines más bellas en un espejo cóncavo son absurdas] (*LBo*, 182). His companion dubiously agrees but protests that he enjoys the entertainment of the Calle del Gato. Estrella admits a similar fascination, going on to define what was to become Valle-Inclán's idiosyncratic aesthetic of modern life, the *esperpento*: 'Deformation is no longer deformation when it adheres to perfect mathematical principles. My present aesthetic is to transform classical norms with the mathematics of the concave mirror' [la deform-ación deja de serlo cuanso está sujeta a una matemática perfecta. Mi estética actual es transformar con matemática de espejo cóncavo las normas clásicas] (*LBo*, 182). The paradox of the assumed veracity and yet often queer effects of reflection is a visual motif that Valle-Inclán also uses in scene 9, when Estrella meets with the Nicaraguan modernist poet Rubén Darío in the Café Colón. The appearance of the café has been distorted by placing mirrors directly opposite each other, so that 'The multiplying mirrors hold melodramatic interest. In their depths the café recedes in extravagant geometric form' [Los espejos multiplicadores están llenos de un interés folletinesco. En su fondo, con una geometría absurda, estravaga el Café] (*LBo*, 160). The manipulation of spatial form by the infinite reflections of the mirrors, a mathematical trick that of course Estrella ironically cannot see, directly anticipates his later statements about the mirrors of the Calle de Gato.

The *esperpento* was to form an art of the grotesque, the carnivalesque and the dehumanized that corresponded to what Valle-Inclán regarded as a specifically national condition, epitomised in the urban context of Madrid. If modern, bour-geois Spain saw itself in the image of the consummate metropolis represented by the Gran Vía, the reflections in the comic mirrors deform such triumphal aspir-ations to reveal the city in all its disoriented, awkward and ridiculous reality. The person who looks in a distorting mirror, suddenly sees all the ludicrousness of his or her everyday pretensions and illusions. For Estrella, and for Valle-Inclán, the predicament of Spain, Madrid and the alienated modern individual was that they were caught in a grotesque affectation of modernity. The only resort, Estrella proposes, is to confront this absurd condition and to respond with self-mockery rather than anguish, to admit to the hilarity that accompanies tragic situations and gives temporary release to their horror or bitterness. In the mock-tragic figure of Estrella himself, then, Valle-Inclán plays homage to another influence of the cinema screen. Estrella is Madrid's Chaplin, a human puppet pathetically caught within a series of absurd misadventures, a lonely clown who exaggerates his own ridiculousness, and a vagabond artist who finds vision in the incongruous and the deformed. Loosely based on Valle-Inclán's close associate Alejandro Sawa, a blind poet who had lived in Paris in the 1880s and 1890s, and who had become a notorious cosmopolitan figure in the literary Madrid of the turn-of-the-century, Estrella embodies at once a posture of anti-heroic bohemianism and an ultimately Spanish absurdity. 'To the street, to the battle, to fight with phantoms!' [¡A la calle, a la batalla, a luchar con fantasmas!], Sawa wrote in his novel *Iluminaciones en sombra* (Illuminations in the shade).[20] Estrella's futile struggles against an inhuman modernity are similarly quixotic, despairing attacks on the shadows and demons that make up his world, and that are ultimately meaningless in the light of day.

Coincident with the growing avant-garde fascination with silent film, cinema was becoming the ultimate embodiment of modern mass culture, dominated by the commercial control of Hollywood. Arturo Casinos Guillén, for example, protesting in 1932 against Hollywood's 'monumental film studios, great factories of celluloid' [monumentales estudios cinematográficos, grandes fábricas de celuloide], stated that they produced only 'a false, insubstantial cinema' [un cinema falso, insubstancial]. The masses, he argued, apathetically consuming the melodramatic fantasies of Hollywood film, 'see in it only a pastime, a distraction, a simple spectacle to sweeten a few hours of their long and monotonous existence' [solo ven en él un pasatiempo, una distracción, un simple espectáculo más que viene a endulzarles unas cuantas horas en su larga y monótona existencia].[21] Cinema for the majority of viewers, he complained, far from an elite aesthetic, was a syrupy opiate to the realities of everyday life. For in the world as it is conceived and presented by Hollywood, another critic fumed, 'there are no unemployed, there is no poverty, or hunger, or strikes; there are no repressions, no oppressed peoples, no bankruptcies'.[22] If the Gran Vía presented modernity as a glossy veneer of pleasure and consumption, so too did its cinemas, the 'optical fairylands' of mass urban society.[23]

In his 1923 novel *Cinelandia*, Ramón Gómez de la Serna presents a mocking parody of Hollywood as a fantastic microcosm of urban, mass-cultural modernity, Cinelandia (Cinemaland), a 'great factory of images' [La gran fábrica de imágenes] (*C*, 60), governed by a thinly veiled caricature of Thomas Edison, 'the great cinematographic exploiter Emerson, emperor of film' [el gran explotador cinematográfico Emerson, emperador de la película] (*C*, 36). Through Gómez de la Serna's Madrilenian lens, however, the landscape of Cinelandia distinctly resembles not so much Hollywood as the Spanish capital. Cinelandia, for example, like Madrid, holds its 'traditional and authentic' [típica y verdadura] (*C*, 98) fiesta every May, marked by an evening of lively and drunken picnicking in the countryside: 'the moonlight picnics were an orgy in which the shadows of the cinema . . . searched for the reality of their reality' [las meriendas bajo la luna eran una orgía en que las sombras de la cinematografía . . . buscaban la realidad de su realidad] (*C*, 97). Moreover, as the fantasy city has no outlying areas or periphery, all are clustered as a city centre, forming a 'nucleus of great buildings' [núcleo de grandes edificios] in an eclectic mix of architectural styles and international fashions. 'The appearance of Cinelandia, from afar', Gómez de la Serna states, 'looked somewhat like Constantinople, combined with Tokyo, traces of Florence and good deal of New York' [El aspecto de Cinelandia, desde lejos, tenía algo de Constantinopla, mezclado de Tokio, con algo de Florencia y con bastante de Nueva York] (*C*, 35). Just as the Gran Vía was the synthetic, international face of modern Madrid, and a concentrated space of pleasure and entertainment, so Cinelandia is 'a false city, invented only for fun' [una ciudad falsa, inventada solo para el juego] (*C*, 35), its panorama resembling 'an immense Luna Park' [un Luna Park inmenso] (*C*, 35).

The inhabitants of Cinelandia, like the city itself, are two-dimensional, caricatures of romantic films and movie gossip. In 'the most fantastic centre of overproduction' [el centro más fabuloso de superproducción] (*C*, 60), all are superficial figures, either mannequins groomed to conform to cinematic types, or chameleons who constantly change in appearance and identity. None have been born in the city, and when they arrive renounce their previous identity, to be made-over and renamed into multiple copies of the icons of the silver screen; starlets, screen goddesses, child actresses, villains, playboys, fat men, screen lovers, etc. The female population, for example, is almost entirely composed of peroxide goddesses or doe-eyed ingenues, who own 'more than a thousand gowns' [más de mil trajes] (*C*, 44) and adopt pseudonyms such as Venus de Plata (Silver Venus). Ridiculing the images of modern femininity constructed by the cinema, Gómez de la Serna at once mimics the cinema's fetishistic objectification of women, and offers an astute comment on women's active engagement in their own commodification. The popular cinema, however, arouses desires that are clichéd and unattainable, ultimately resulting not in pleasure but in dissatisfaction. Venus de Plata, for example, tells her admirer that she will never fall in love as it could only be a disappointment 'after seeing the fables of our films' [después de ver las fábulas de nuestras películas] (*C*, 56), while a listless actress, bored by perpetual indulgence, 'surrenders herself to opium and morphine' [se entrega al opio y la morfina] (*C*, 75).

The spaces of cinema are constructed through projection and spectatorship, and in *Cinelandia* Gómez de la Serna employs similar techniques, creating the metropolis of dreams from a cinematic montage of successive images, and critiquing Hollywood with its own tools. Metaphors of eyes and vision, and of light and shadow, as in *Luces de bohemia*, pervade the novel. 'Cinelandia's catalogue of eyes was extraordinary' [El repertorio cinelandés de ojos era extraordinario] (*C*, 122), Gómez de la Serna states at one point, referring with heavy satire to a popular magazine article listing the cocktail of eye colours (including cognac, rum, peppermint, blue gin and champagne) to be seen on the street. The 'cinematic luminosity' [luminosidad cinemática] (*C*, 99) of the city is blinding however: 'Under the powerful lights of the great Cinelandia studios, the eyes gradually lost their intensity' [Bajo la luz potente de gran Estudio de Cinelandia los ojos iban perdiendo intensidad] (*C*, 103). Unable to see beyond the beams of the camera or the projector, the inhabitants of the film city, and the consumers of its productions, know only a world of illusions.

The power of Cinelandia, and that on which it itself depends for existence, is its completely self-contained isolation from the wider world. Cinelandia can only survive whilst the consuming world public, wilfully blind to the fabrications of sets and screen projections, accepts the two-dimensionality of the world of cinema as reality. As Siegfried Kracauer states, 'film demands that the world it reflects be the only one; it should be wrested from every three-dimensional surrounding, or it will fail as an illusion'.[24] When early film shorts were included within variety or *género chico* programmes, for example, their theatricality was emphasised by the fragmentary, local succession of acts and made obvious. By the 1920s, however, modes of presentation and reception had become more standardized. With the development of movie theatres in their own right, film screenings were no longed combined with live performance, and while audiences remained 'culturally and historically specific', they had nevertheless developed a relatively subjective and passive form of spectatorship to the narrative logic of classical cinema.[25] The picture palaces of the Gran Vía absorbed their audience into 'an autonomous fictional world', one that encouraged identification with its illusions rather than detachment from them.[26] Similarly, the illusion of modernity presented by the street itself, worked because its tall white façades acted as screens for the projection of pleasure and fantasy, hiding the reality beyond them. Like Cinelandia, the Gran Vía pretended to be a metropolitan Madrid in microcosm, an instantiation of modernity that refused the city beyond. A decade later, its cultural identity as icon of Madrid's cosmopolitan modernity would be ironically reversed as, standing immutable under the persistent bombing of Franco's Nationalist forces, the Telefónica was taken to the hearts of the people of the city, a symbol of Madrilenian resistance to constant siege and attack.

-6-

Urban Cosmorama

'Take refuge in the frivolity of street life' [Sálvate en la frivolidad de la vida callejera], Ramón Gómez de la Serna states at one point in his autobiography.[1] By the 1920s Madrid was fast becoming a socially magnetic capital of modernity, increasingly secular and cosmopolitan. *Castizo* festivity, however, epitomised by the fiesta of San Isidro, or the *verbenas* of San Antonio, San Juan, San Pedro, and La Paloma, remained a significant aspect of social and cultural self-identity in the expanding and modernising city. Importantly incorporated *into* the everyday life of urban modernity rather than regarded as a nostalgic tradition that was opposed it, the *verbena* became a hybrid space in which the persistence of *castizo* identity alongside cosmopolitan modernity was overtly articulated. Advertising posters from the period, for example, present the *verbena* as a social and public space of modern vitality and change in which traditionally regional and folkloric images coincide with signs of modernity, notably in mechanical fairground rides, urban buildings and modish young women. Writers and artists, moreover, embraced the public festivity of carnival and comedy as an instinctive and vital force in response to what many modernist intellectuals regarded as the mechanicalism of the educated bourgeoisie. If the fiestas and *verbenas* were a common feature in nineteenth-century representations of Madrid, amongst the avant-garde of the early twentieth century they stimulated an aesthetic of the farcical carnivalesque or the ludic vernacular that was almost ubiquitous.

Carnival of Modernity

In 1928, José Ortega y Gasset organised an exhibition of paintings by a young Galician painter, Maruja Mallo, in the offices of the *Revista de Occidente*. The works were arranged into two groups; kaleidoscopic, carnivalesque scenes under the heading of '*Verbenas*', and surreal images of mannequins and other objects described as '*Estampas Populares*'. Opening to great critical acclaim, Gómez de la Serna described the paintings as 'a step forward, a new departure, a signpost' for a new generation in Spanish art, and Mallo herself as 'Queen of the Verbena'.[2] Dramatically juxtaposing the folkloric, Madrilenian fiesta with the technological, cosmopolitan influence of cinema, however, the exhibition again displayed a city of two extremes, in which both its urban landscape and the popular imagination were divided between the twin yet paradoxical ideologies of modernity and *lo castizo*.

Arriving in Madrid from Galicia in 1922 to study at the Escuela de Bellas Artes de San Fernando, like Gómez de la Serna Mallo immersed herself in the city's street-life, particularly that of its older *barrios*.[3] The writer Concha Méndez, for example, recalling their walks together through the city, states:

> We would go to the Prado Museum . . . to the street parties and to the slums of Madrid. We would take walks to see the colourful characters that passed by illuminated by in the light of the street lamps. Women were not allowed in the taverns; and in protest we would press up against the windows to watch what was happening inside. On Sunday afternoons we would go to the Del Norte station, to watch the trains, the people departing and arriving, and travellers bidding farewell.
>
> [Íbamos al Museo del Prado . . . a las verbenas y a los barrios bajos de Madrid. Nos paseábamos para ver aquellos personajes tan pintorescos que pasaban a nuestro lado iluminados por los faroles de la calles. Estaba prohibido que las mujeres entraran a las tabernas; y nosotros, para protestar, nos pegábamos a los ventanales a mirar lo que pasaba dentro. Los domingos por la tarde íbamos a la Estación del Norte, a ver a la gente que va y que llega, a los viajeros con sus despedidas y los trenes].[4]

Observing the types and rhythms of the street through detached *flânerie*, the two women are here fascinated by both the *castizo* city of *verbenas* and bars, a picturesque scene viewed through the medium of lamp-light or a window frame, and the modern urban space of the railway station, with its crowds of passengers in transit and the trains that carry them to and fro across Spain and the continent. Accompanied by the sculptor Alberto Sánchez and artist Benjamín Palencia, Mallo also explored the newer working-class areas on the southern outskirts of the city. 'They invited me to see the sourthern zone' [Me invitaron a conocer la Zona Sur], she remembered, describing a journey to the suburb of Vallecas. What immediately captures Mallo's aesthetic imagination, however, is the station from which they leave:

> Atocha, born in 1892, an architectural and urban landmark. We would enter the building, where traffic lights presided with their functional expressions, a code that we could not decipher but which for us held a magical attraction . . . beckoning us to walk on the iron pathways. This unique morphological feature of transport, was our flight forwards; this desire to walk on the parallel metal tracks, would foreshadow our ventures across the frontiers of the world.
>
> [Atocha, nacida en 1892, pieza clave arquitectónica y urbanística. Penetrábamos en dicho edificio, donde los semáforos presidían con sus expresiones funcionales, clave no descifrable para nosotros, pero mágica para nuesta atración . . . seduciéndonos caminar

sobre los caminos de hierro. Esta singular tendencia morfológica de transporte, era nuestra fuga hacia adelante; este deseo de andar sobre las paralelas metálicas, sería una previsión de atravesar las fronteras del mundo].[5]

An iron temple to modern technology and communication, Atocha becomes a phantasmagoria for the three artists. With Futurist exuberance, Mallo fantasises becoming one with the train, rushing along the iron tracks not with rational functionality but limitless possibility.

At the Escuela de Bellas Artes she had also quickly become friends with Salvador Dalí, and through him the burgeoning avant-garde of Madrid's all-male student college, the Residencia des Estudientes, among them Federico Garcia Lorca and Luis Buñuel. With them she formed part of what she later described as a 'nocturnal association of brothers' [noctámbula asociación de cofrades], meeting to wander the city, fascinated by the surreal images that the moonlight and shadows of the streets at night brought forth.[6] Dalí illustrated these walks in a number of sketches of the city under the heading of *Madrid Scenes*: cubist-style collages in black and grey ink of street corners and cafés at night, surrounded by alienating buildings, lurking figures and stray cats. Mallo's representation of Madrid in her '*Verbenas*', however, would be very different, focused on the colour of rural and folk tradition, but also pervaded by the electric light, speed and mechanical vibrancy of modernity. In a lecture given in 1937, Mallo recalled that 'What struck me most at that time is reflected in my work: the street scene . . . the pattern of everyday life: the diversity of beings and objects'.[7] The series of four images, *La Verbena* (1927), *La Verbena De Pascua* (1927), *Kermesse* (1928) and *Verbena* (1928), depict the carnivalesque vitality of the local street fairs of the various Madrid *barrios*, in which past and present, tradition and modernity merge, as images of festival folklore, *castizo* dress and decorated food-stalls form a collage of simultaneity with modern figures, cars and machine rides.

In the '*Verbenas*' Mallo presents Madrid in the image of street frivolity and fiesta, Gómez de la Serna, for example, suggesting that they depict the entire metropolis as a fairground, a 'Verbena Capital'.[8] Describing the *verbena* as an alternative universe, she states, '[t]he entire atmosphere is loaded with magic surprises and messages . . . [f]or 5 cents you have the planets and constellations within reach of your hand'.[9] It is above all a landscape packed with simultaneous images and fantastic objects, 'a marvellous factory of things total and multiple', everyday things brought together in the 'transforming' and mirroring' space of 'A Verbena'.[10] Much is traditional and folkloric, but also pervaded by the modern. In the first painting, *La Verbena*, for example, from 1927 (Fig. 6), set against the mountains of the Guadarrama, provincial elements are clearly manifest, described in her 1937 essay as the 'crowds from around the capital who came laden with branches, toys, almonds, rattles, alms, jugs, jars, mats, baskets, wickerwork,

Figure 6 Maruja Mallo, *La Verbena* (1927), Centro de Arte Reína Sofía

marzipan, all made from the land, the growing things and the skill of the peoples of Alcalá, Avila, Toledo, Colmenar, Cuenca and Tarancón'.[11] These are juxtaposed, however, with the urban generation of the machine age. San Isidro's 'angels' are buxom and emancipated young women, with short skirts and plunging necklines that are eyed appreciatively by a group of sailors.

The gradually changing scene of urban carnival depicted over the period of the four paintings, thus also implies a subordination of traditional and religious elements to secularised festivity and the mass productions of modern life. The two 1928 paintings are dominated by mechanical carrousels and Ferris wheels, on which urban pleasure-seekers rather than traditional local figures experience modernity as a constantly spinning and circular existence, a world in which the forces of space are centrifugal and condensed in the city. The jollity of the pictures is partly ironic, and the atmosphere of parody, ridiculousness and frivolity becomes an ambiguous metaphor of modernity. The impressions recorded by the second section of the 1928 exhibition, such as the '*Estampas Cinemáticas*' portraying 'terror-stricken squares, the clamour of discordant mechanisms, the human beings, the skyscrapers, the electric signs', can thus perhaps be seen not so much as opposed to, but rather in dialectical relation with the '*Verbenas*'.[12] Rather than a lively vision of *castizo* merriment, the 'Verbenas' perhaps, as one perceptive critic noted, ultimately 'provided an extra-territorial refuge for the artist unconsciously out of sympathy with the world in which she lived'.[13]

If there is a thematically picturesque or *costumbrismo* element to Mallo's *'Verbenas'*, however, there is also a fascination with modernity as form and aesthetic. Rafael Alberti states of the Madrid avant-garde of the 1920s, 'The cinema influenced us considerably . . . An apparent mechanistic confusion disturbed us' [El cine nos influía mucho . . . Una aparente confusión mecanista nos turbaba], continuing, 'Maruja, reflects this in her *verbenas* and urban scenes' [Maruja, en sus verbenas y estampas urbanas lo refleja].[14] The film director Benito Perojo had interestingly recently included a sequence shot at a Madrid fiesta in his film *la condesa María* (1927), exploiting the effect of merry-go-rounds whirling amidst a scene of traditional local dances and dress.[15] The medium of film provided Perojo with the means to register the spectacular vitality of the fair through a thematic and stylistic juxtaposition of tradition and modernity, historical exactitude and experimental cinematic technique, a successful combination that he continued in his 1935 adaptation of Bretón and De la Vega's *La Verbena de la Paloma*. The balance of the past and the modern, and the apt association of fairground and film, was widely recognised, Antonio Barbero for the newspaper *ABC*, for example, commenting that, 'the historical evocation of characters and customs is successfully combined with artistic techniques specific to the cinema: the play of shapes and the positioning of the machine' [La evocación histórica de tipos y costumbres viene felizamente conjugada con lo que es técnica artística privativa del cinema: el juego de las figuras y la colocación de la máquina].[16] In Mallo's *'Verbenas'*, the mechanical rides and electric lights similarly create a cinematic whirl of activity and colour that upturn conventional perspective, as if the viewer himself is observing the carnival from another disorientating and dizzying ride. She presents the *verbena* as a space of specifically Madrilenian urbanity, a sensual cacophony of simultaneous impressions that evokes at once *lo castizo* and a cinematic modernity.

In her presentation of the *verbena* as a site of clashing cultures and styles in both theme and form, Mallo's concept of popular festival follows the ideas of Mikhail Bakhtin on folk culture, and particularly carnival, as inherently 'heteroglossic' and polymorphic.[17] Bakhtin's definition of the early modern carnival is significant, moreover, for emphasising the detachment of the carnival spirit proper from the calendar as laid down by either Church or state. As Michael Holquist notes, '[t]he sanction for carnival derives ultimately not from a calendar prescribed by church or state, but from a force that preexists priests and kings and to whose superior power thay are actually deferring when they appear to be licensing carnival'.[18] The localised *verbenas*, similarly, are periods of collective festivity that involve little reverance for the authority of the Church, despite the religious myths attached to them. 'They are a Pagan revelation', Mallo states, 'and express a lack of harmony with the existing order':

> On these commemorative occasions the common people come together. They take mythology and the saints as an excuse for communal jollification. They are not moved by the slightest respect for religion, but on the contrary parody the heavenly order and the infernal hierarchy, disguising themselves with the elements and attributes of divine and devilish figures.[19]

Bakhtin was highly sceptical about modernist idealisation of the carnival spirit, and the appropriation of folk culture by the intellectual elite as a means of regenerating human freedom and spontaneous cultural production in the age of bourgeois modernity. Moreover, as much as a subversive reversal of authoritative social structures, he also recognised it to be an obstacle to actual social revolution, operating rather as a safety valve for the social order, a sanctioned and thus controlled space for the common people to release energies that might otherwise be channelled into insurgency. It is significant however, that Mallo's comments are retrospective, written soon after her exile to Buenos Aires, and in the year that the pre-Lenten fiesta of *Carnaval* was banned by General Franco, who obviously found it subversive enough. When Mallo claims that 'In popular art we find the strife of Spain', implicit in her words is that the fiesta, and certainly the *verbena*, neither a national nor in the popular imagination particularly religious celebration, did not honour the combined forces of the Franco regime. Looking back, the *verbena* could become for Mallo a standard of the common people and of a frivolity that resists the dictates of social and religious order. The vernacular of the *verbena*, to which Mallo had responded in her early twenties, offered an artfully resistant popular culture of idiosyncratic social identity, symbolising a shared landscape of the Madrid street that had been lost in exile.

Ludic Streets

What perhaps most distinguishes the modernist experimentation of Madrid-based writers and artists in the first decades of the twentieth century is, as Derek Harris describes, 'a confusion, rather than a fusion' of European movements arriving belatedly and thus all at once as influences on the Spanish capital.[20] Gómez de la Serna's allegiances were varied, and his own style idiosyncratic. His status within Spanish and European literary history suffered from almost total neglect in the second half of the twentieth century, yet for a time he was one of the most provocative and notorious writers of European modernism, actively promoting an aesthetic avant-garde within the Spanish capital. In 1909, for example, he translated Marinetti's *Futurist Manifesto*, published in Madrid one month after its first publication in French in Paris. Pablo Neruda described him as 'the great figure of surrealism within all countries', and Octavio Paz recalled that 'there was a moment in which modernity spoke through the mouth of Ramón Gómez de la Serna'.[21]

Gómez de la Serna's urban aesthetic, although less concerned with a critique of the 'starving' than with eulogising the 'absurd' and the 'brilliant' of the Madrilenian phantasmagoria, is not dissimilar to that of Valle-Inclán, questioning conventional perception in the manner of a cinematic carnivalesque. Through the technique of the *greguería*, fleeting images stimulated by the experience of the ever-moving city, in the form of witty metaphors that fragment our assumptions about the meanings of space and time, he makes the familiar strange. What perhaps most distinguishes Gómez de la Serna from Valle-Inclán, however, is his ebullient optimism, which accepts the incongruity and the chaos of modern life as the image, not so much of the grotesque, but of the frivolous. Ortega y Gasset described him, alongside James Joyce and Marcel Proust, as epitomising an avant-garde 'super-realism', in which the mundane and inconsequential was magnified to the level of the transcendent.[22] Certainly the trivial objects and everyday practices of the city never failed to capture his capricious eye, or to be endowed with a heightened and often incongruous significance.

Gómez de la Serna's technique for revealing the 'superreality' of the everyday, was the *greguería*, brief, aphoristic metaphors that defamiliarise and explode conventional understandings of space, time and identity, 'the attempt to define that which cannot be defined, to capture the fleeting'.[23] It is the *greguería* that dominates both his fictional and non-fictional writing on the city, a method for expressing the simultaneous, multi-perspectival impressions of the street in all their multiple and absurd realities. Collapsing objective reality with the often irrational associations of subjective perception, he produces Madrid as a conjunction of material and psychological realities. His fascination with at once the history and the modern technologies of the city, with its built map and its imaginative representation, with its spectacle and with its mysteries, results in a new literary cartography of the city, a mental map of Madrid.

Ramón Gómez de la Serna did for Madrid something similar to what Walter Benjamin did for Paris; he revealed its unconscious life, its spatial psychodynamics, the prehistory of its modernity. If Madrid possessed a *flâneur* in the truest sense then Gómez de la Serna was it. He epitomised the confrontation of the aesthetic temperament of the dandy artist with the crowd of urban modernity, revelling in the spectacle of the street and the erotics of the object. Keith Tester, for example, describes the *flâneur* in terms highly applicable to Gómez de la Serna as,

> the individual soverign of the order of things, who, as a poet or as the artist, is able to transform faces and things so that for him they have only that meaning which he attributes to them. He therefore treats the objects of the city with a somewhat detached

attitude (an attitude which is only a short step away from isolation and alienation . . .). The *flâneur* is the secret spectator of the spectacle of the spaces and places of the city. Consequently, *flâneurie* can, after Baudelaire, be understood as the activity of the sovereign spectator going about the city in order to find the things which will occupy his gaze and thus complete his otherwise incomplete identity; satisfy his otherwise dissatisfied existence; replace the sense of bereavement with a sense of life.[24]

Unlike Baudelaire, Gómez de la Serna responded to the city with frivolity rather than spleen, but he nevertheless required it for existence, Madrid becoming an illuminated screen for the projection of his identity. The object as *greguería*, he stated 'refers to me, who changed its meaning, who converted it into something it was not'.[25] Through the technique of the *greguería*, he moved from simply observing the spaces and objects of the city to merging himself with them.

In his quasi-fictional urban guide, *Historia de la Puerta del Sol*, written in 1920, Gómez de la Serna celebrates Madrid's central square as the iconic locus of at once the celebrated past of the city, and of its modernity. Originally the city's eastern gate, it was the first area to be illuminated by gas and then electric street-lighting, and the terminus of the city's tram and metro networks. *Historia de la Puerta del Sol* presents an account of its origins and architectural development, anecdotes of the major social and political events to which it played host, the arrival of gas and electric street-lighting, its development as the terminus of the city's tram and later metro networks, as well as a guide to its buildings, cafes and entertainments. With the approach of the present day, however, the style of Gómez de la Serna's narrative alters from Baedeker-like narration to an increasingly fragmentary mode of observation. Attempting to capture the square as it is constantly practised, perceived and represented by a myriad of users, the text offers cinematic snapshots, visual images that evoke the multiple resonance of its social and sensual spatiality (Fig. 7).

In the penultimate chapters, for example, a collage of visual images evoke the vibrant, multiple stimulations of the square through a cinematic combination of montage and simultaneity. 'Algunas horas de la Puerta del Sol' ('Some hours of the Puerta del Sol'), is composed as a symphony of the visual rhythms of the square over twenty-four hours. Beginning in the early morning before dawn, the *madrugada*, it stands quiet and empty: 'The air has turned so fluid that you can hear the whistles from the trains in all the stations. It has been left without trams and the old tracks look like thin streams' [Se torno tan fluido el aire que se oyen los pitidos de los trenes de todas las estaciones. Se ha quedado sin tranvías, y se ve que los rieles paracen delgados arroyuelos] (*HPS*, 95). Daybreak brings the first movement, and taxi-cars that illuminate floating oil fumes with their headlights, 'in the heart of which lives the candle of the night, butterflies of oil floating in the night' [en cuyo fondo vive aún la lamparilla de la noche, las mariposas de aceite

Figure 7 Enrique Martínez Cubells, *Puerta de Sol* (1900), Museo Municipal de Madrid

flotantes en la noche] (*HPS*, 96). Then follow, at seven and eight o'clock, street vendors, school children, doctors and clerks on their way to work, as the cafés and *churrerías* open and breakfast begins to be served. By nine o'clock the square has become a vast terminus, teaming with human traffic, and 'the Puerta del Sol is like a busy central station that is coming fully to life' [la Puerta del Sol parece una estación de gran tráfico que se despierta completamente] (*HPS*, 99).

The square really takes on its identity as the asphalt playground of the city between the hours of six and nine o'clock, 'the hours when people take their walks through the Puerta del Sol, and there is a full house in the great cinema of life' [las horas álgidas del paseo por la Puerta del Sol y del lleno en su gran cinematógrafo de la vida] (*HPS*, 103). For Gómez de la Serna, no city is comparable to Madrid at this time of day: 'Shadows, and young people pass by . . . Cheerful silhouettes . . . Everyone is out for a stroll, to enjoy the delights of life' [Pasan sombras, gentes mozas . . . Son siluetas joviales. Todas las ciudades tienen las calles más desoladas a esta hora. . . . Hay paseíto, y delectación de la vida en el andar de todos] (*HPS*, 104). *Flânerie*, for Gómez de la Serna, would seem less inherently Parisian than it is indisputably Madrilenian. People flood into the theatres and cinemas, and then out again, and the metro becomes busy with trains leaving for the residential suburbs. Finally, with the departure of the last train of the night, the city sleeps, in the stillness of the few hours of the *madrugada*.

'Greguerías de la Puerta del Sol' ('Aphorisms of the Puerta del Sol'), resists conventional linear temporality to present disconnected and often surreal images that evoke the square's multiple, simultaneous animation:

> Sometimes horses pass walking like dancers, others bulls. . . . There are times when the Ministry of the Interior seems like a piece of well-finished furniture. . . . The women walk through the Puerta del Sol with smiles on their faces, from all the compliments they receive. . . . Many men, with a cone or great cylinder of papers in their hands.
> [A veces pasan caballos que andan como una bailarina, y otros que son como toros . . . El Ministerio de Gobernación hay momentos en que parece un mueble muy bien acabado . . . La mujeres, de tantos piropos como las dicen, pasan la Puerta del Sol sonriendo. . . . Muchos hombres, con un cuchuro o cilindro grande de papeles en la mano] (*HPS*, 113)

Presiding over the scene is, significantly, Madrid's great clock, erected in Sol in 1867 over the Ministry of the Interior, yet repeatedly described as notoriously unreliable: 'Why does that clock with its luminous hours and hands always say half-past three? [¿Por qué en ese reloj de horas y manillas luminosas son siempre las tres y media?] (*HPS*, 116). As the locus of past and present, a transport hub that conveys people rapidly in and out of the city, and a space in which, dazzling constantly with an electric glow, it is never night, the Puerta del Sol collapses time.

If the Puerta del Sol displayed the social, technological and consumerist aspects of Madrid's modernity, then the fleamarket was its dumping ground, an abject space of rubbish and used goods. In *El Rastro* (1915), the text with which Gómez de la Serna introduced the *greguería*, attention to realist detail is exaggerated and transformed into a fascination and delight in things in all their surreal triviality and ludic absurdity. 'The Rastro is not a symbolic place, nor simply a local spot' [El Rastro no es un lugar simbólico ni es un simple rincón local], he states in the prologue to the book, but the site of an urban wasteland common to all cities, spaces in which 'old and useless junk accumulates' [se aglomeran los trastos viejos e inservibles].[26] Far from a wasteland, however, it is full of fragmentary, abandoned objects that have been collected to be sold on.

In the transforming space of the Rastro, the broken and the unwanted are suddenly seen in a new light, and 'things' take on a new fascination: 'And what things! Carnal, deeply intimate, heart-rending, gentle, distant, close, distinct: things that are revealing in their insignificance, in their simplicity, in their mundaneity' [¡Y qué cosas! Cosas carnales, entrañables, desgarrados, clementes, lejanas, cercanas, distintas: cosas reveladores en su insignificancia, en su llaneza, en su mundanidad].[27] The art form that captures and expresses the incongruous poetry of this proliferation of conventionally prosaic yet surreal things is the *greguería*, for,

> The Rastro is above all, more than a place of things, a place of images and associations of ideas, associations of emotions, of things suffered, tender and intimate, which, in order not to betray themselves, once formed, disintegrate into white, transparent, floating and volatile ironies.
>
> [el Rastro es sobre todo, más que un lugar de cosas, un lugar de imágenes y de asociaciones de ideas, imágenes, asociaciones sensibles, sufridas, tiernas, interiores, que para no traicionarse, tan pronto como se forman y a continuación, se deforman en blancas, transparentes, aéreas y volanderas ironías] [28]

Gómez de la Serna's Madrid writings are an attempt to capture these odds and scraps of perception and association, which flutter like rags across the city landscape.

Akin to Walter Benjamin in his intoxication with the obsolete and insignificant objects of everyday life, Ramón Gómez de la Serna, as both walker and writer of Madrid, was a curious rag-picker, his aesthetic feeding off a city that he recreated from its own fragments. '*Rastro*' means 'trace' and the fleamarket is one of the spaces in which the traces of the fleeting and the evanescent, those aspects of the modern that modernism so desperately attempts to capture, can be found, retained in the past-life of objects. A passionate collector of such objects, in his study in Madrid and later Buenos Aires, Gómez de la Serna cherished a multitude of bizarre things that included a life-size mannequin, a carnival drum, a street-lamp, distorting mirrors, globes and mechanical toys. Benjamin describes collecting as 'a form of practical memory', in which the collection forms 'an encyclopaedia of all knowledge of the epoch, the landscape, the industry, and the owner from which it comes'.[29] Gómez de la Serna's Madrid writings are diverse and extensive, ranging from studies of specific sites, such as the Puerta del Sol, the Rastro fleamarket, or the Café Pombo which he appropriated for his own, notorious *tertulia*, to the circus, the cinema, even the city's urinals. A surreal form of *costumbrismo*, they present not simply a panorama of the map of the city, however, or even a palimpsest of its history, but instead create it as an entire universe. 'Ramón has made an inventory of the world', Jorge Luis Borges stated in 1925, continuing that, 'Such an abundance is not in harmony nor can it be simplified through synthesis, it is closer to the cosmorama or the atlas than the total vision of life so sought after by theologians and creators of systems'.[30] Gómez de la Serna's 'world' was ultimately Madrid, his writings offering minutely detailed and illuminated pictures of the city rather than a totalising panorama. Together, however, the simultaneous fragments form a system of connections, with at their centre the degree zero of the Puerta del Sol.

'All of us in Madrid are convinced that Madrid is a chimera', Gómez de la Serna wrote from exile in Buenos Aires in 1949.[31] 'I do not believe in the Madrid of some ultraprovincial novelists who applied their own newly arrived surprises to the most intricately coloured city of the world', he continued, 'They lack ingenious impulses, spirited whims'. The comment is a nostalgic eulogy to the kaleidoscopic, frivolous and gregarious streetlife that he regarded as specific to Madrid and no other modern city. He wrote obsessively, over a period of half a century, on all aspects of the space, culture and phenomena of the city, combining the ambulatory reverie of the *flâneur* with a distinct focus on the social, topographical and mythological landscape of the Spanish capital. Chronicler *par excellence* of its genus loci, for Gómez de la Serna the practices, affective associations and, above all, the *things* of Madrid, were inseparable from his own identity as its observer. Francisco Umbral, writes that, 'Madrid is Ramón's great work, the recurrent theme of his life'.[32] Madrid's fascination with its own image, as it emanated from its streets, cafés and stage, pervades representations of the city throughout the nineteenth and early twentieth centuries; from the conservative sensibility yet reformist idealism of Ramón Mesonero Romanos, to the panoramic and systemic perspective of Benito Pérez Galdós, the sociological impressionism of Pío Baroja, the lively nostalgia of Carlos Arniches, and the indefatigable exuberance and surreal imagination of Ramón Gómez de la Serna. Without Galdós, Baroja, Mesonero and Arniches, Umbral again states, the city would not be so graphically illustrated, 'but without Ramón it would not be so dark, so poetically vague' [pero sin Ramón no estaría tan oscuro, tan vago de poesía].[33]

–7–

Epilogue

Madrid finally fell to Franco's Nationalist forces in March 1939, after almost three years of siege, starvation and bombardment. The decades that followed were characterised by misery, repression, strict censorship and, as Camilo José Cela writes in his novel *La colmena* ('The Hive'), a 'yawning, remorseless emptiness'.[1] Under the policies of the dictatorship, development was brought to a halt and Spain distanced from modernising Europe, as a counterfeit and homogenising national traditionalism was promulgated by the early Francoist propaganda machine. At the centre of this ideology of fake *hispanidad* stood Madrid, its own cultural myths of identity repressed or subsumed under the New State's decision to make the city the capital of its Castilian-based nationalism. Economic need resulted in a less isolationist stance in the 1950s, facilitated by political agreement with the United States, but it was not until 1975 and the death of the *Caudillo* that Spain began its transformation into what would become 'surely the most modern of societies'.[2] '"Madrid is the centre of the universe and everybody comes here to have fun"', announced Almodóvar, describing the premise of his film *Laberinto de pasiones* ('Labyrinth of Passion', 1982).[3] A statement that he claimed was made 'in one of the least imaginative moments of my life', it has yet come to define and shape the city's contemporary identity.

Manuel Castells provides a detailed summary of the beginnings of a new urbanity in Madrid in his case-study of the urban protest movements of 1970s Madrid in his *The City and the Grassroots* (1983).[4] The development of Madrid as an industrial city in the 1960s had brought with it a massive increase in immigration. New housing provision was concentrated largely on the urban periphery, in a concentration of poor-quality high-rise accommodation blocks that offered few of the basic social amenities of urban life. By 1974, as Castells records, 54 per cent of the Madrid population lived in sub-standard housing, often little more than shanty-housing.[5] The result was collective urban protest under the Madrid Citizen Movement, in which 'social revolt and spatial innovation' were brought together in public demand for, in Lefebvre's words, 'their 'right to the city'; for better quality and more affordable housing, improved infrastructure and neighbourhood services, the protection and conservation of the historic centre of the city, and an improved social and cultural life.[6] The local authorities responded, replacing the demolition schemes so beloved by 1960s and 70s urban planning across Europe with programmes of rehabilitation, and developing new low-cost housing with improved urban amenities and services, including open space. 'The city itself changed', Castells declares, 'neighbourhoods organized celebrations; cultural and popular traditions were restored and others were invented in the newly built urban areas; a whole network of associations and activities were established; the metropolitan area became a public place, enriched with street life, cultural activities, and community and city gatherings'.[7] The return of many of the local fiestas focused community identity, and reawakened the specific cultural sense of place belonging to the different districts and *barrios*.

After the electoral victory of the PSOE in 1979, the new Socialist mayor of Madrid, Enrique Tierno Galván, set about the modern revitalisation of the city's popular customs, reinstating the celebrations for *Carnaval*, instigating a new series of summer art festivals the *Veranos de la Villa*, and generally declaring that the city was indeed a space to have fun. Paralleling the process of cultural rememory in the urban communities' reclaiming of their local identities and traditions, a new youth culture lost no time in taking him at his word, parodying the fake national identity promoted by Franco and experimenting with all previous taboos in a frenzy of hedonism, sexual promiscuity and nocturnal excess. Madrid was 'a city gone crazy' Almodóvar states, describing his arrival in the city from La Mancha in 1969, 'that had clandestine fun under the shadow of the dictatorship and was getting ready to shift into a rhythm of vertigo as soon as the nightmare was over'.[8] The Madrid 'scene', or *movida madrileña* as it was later called, of the late 1970s and early 1980s, was headed by an artistic coterie who outrageously paraded their self-claimed identity as 'the moderns'.[9] 'We had no memory; we imitated everything we liked and had a great time doing it', Almodóvar recalls, '[t]here wasn't the slightest sense of solidarity, nor any political, social or generational feelings, and the more we plagiarized, the more authentic we were'.[10] In a revision of Francoist ideology through kitsch parody of the stereotypical images of Spanish culture, the *movida* was the city's 'New Golden Age' of 'pop, punk, comics and general frivolity', epitomised in the brash exuberance of Almodóvar's first feature-length film, *Pepi Luci Bom y otras chicas del Montón* ('Pepi Luci Bom and other Girls Like Mom', 1980).[11]

Almodóvar's focus in his early films has consistently been the everyday life of Madrid during the end of the dictatorship, the Transition and the new democracy, the changing social and political environment reflected in the transformation of the physical landscape from the shabbiness of the late 1970s to the vibrant Euro-city of the 1990s. Central to his conception of the city remains the dialectic of modernity and local tradition that pervades its social, spatial and symbolic form. 'Just as people are composed of thousands of facets (many of them contradictory)', he states, for me this city contains a thousand cities in one. Eight of them have appeared in my movies. Pepi *Luci Bom and other Girls Like Mom* combined the rustic with the metropolitan. . . . The sets also showed this same polarization: the street corners in the working-class district of *Prosperidad*, the New Yorkish profile of the Azca, the shops and bars along Princesa, the Rastro . . . In *Labyrinth of Passion* Madrid becomes explosive and cosmopolitan, the nerve center of the world, where everything was happening and nobody cared. Prostitution and devoutness in *Dark Habits* . . . The desolation of the housing projects of *La Concepción* and the bottomless sea of the M-30 in *What Have I Done*. The inscrutable Viaducto de la Vistillas, the Casa de Campo and a Legazpi slaughterhouse in *Matador*. The sweaty summer nights, the patios and urinals in *Law of Desire*. And a freshly made-up Madrid, with the telephone company and Gran Vía in the background (one of my favourite landscapes) in *Woman on the Verge of a Nervous Breakdown*.[12]

This new cityscape is familiar, a mix of the provincial and the metropolitan, the *castizo* and the cosmopolitan, of chaotic vibrancy at its centre and desolate expanse on its periphery, with the Gran Vía again the cosmetic face of modernity. Across the films the architecture of a new Madrid, the skyscrapers of the Torre Picasso, the Torre España, the FNAC building in the Plaza Callao or the Torres Kio (the city's new 'gateway'), stands alongside an older cultural landscape of the Rastro, the Plaza de la Cebada and the Puerta de Alcalá.

By the end of the 1980s, just as the Madrid art scene was gaining international recognition it was already beginning to reach exhaustion. The flamboyant display of youthful rebellion no longer seeming so meaningful under the established democracy, nor so much fun as AIDS began to rear its head, the city indeed seemed 'on the verge of a nervous breakdown'. After the break with the past that characterised the modernity of the *movida*, Almodóvar's more recent films offer a subtler, self-reflexive consideration of Madrid's contemporary landscape that looks back on its own passage to modernity. Stuck in a taxi amidst the teeming streets of Madrilenian nightlife, a young man born into the silent streets of the dictatorship tells his new-born son at the end of *Carne Tremula* ('Live Flesh', 1997): 'In Spain, we stopped being scared a long time ago'. It is in *Todo sobre mi madre* ('All About My Mother', 1999), however, set in Barcelona, that we find an image perhaps most suggestive of the cultural history of modern Madrid, when, in a repetition of Almodóvar's description of the *movida*, the transsexual La Agrado tells a gathered theatre audience: 'You are more authentic . . . the more you resemble what you've dreamed you are'. In this subversion of the Francoist myth of an 'authentic' Spain, Almodóvar captures the performativity and urban imaginary that characterises and brings together both *castizo* and modern Madrid, both memory and fantasy. *Carne Tremula* and *Todo sobre mi madre* close with the birth of a new generation, and each film looking back to the past is thus also a foundation for the present, for as Almodóvar states, '[l]ike my characters, Madrid has a history: but the past is not enough because the future still excites it'.[13]

Notes

Chapter 1 Introduction: The Castizo Metropolis

1. *The Guardian*, January 19, 2002.
2. Luis Martín-Santos, *Tiempo de Silencio* (Barcelona: Editorial Seix Barral, 1974).
3. Pedro Almodóvar, *The Patty Diphusa Stories*, trans. Kirk Anderson (London: Faber and Faber, 1992), 92.
4. Richard Ford, *Gatherings from Spain* (London: Pallas Athene 2000), 15.
5. Alain de Botton, *The Art of Travel* (London: Hamish Hamilton, 2002), 104.
6. Ibid., 108.
7. H. V. Morton, *A Stranger in Spain* (London: Methuen, 2002), 3–4.
8. Georg Simmel, 'The Metropolis and Mental Life' (1903), in D. Frisby and M. Featherstone (eds), *Simmel on Culture* (London: Sage, 1997), 174–85.
9. Walter Benjamin, *The Arcades Project*, trans. Howard Eiland and Kevin McLaughlin (Cambridge, Mass.: Harvard University Press, 1999).
10. Raymond Williams, *The Country and the City* (London: Chatto and Windus, 1973) and *The Politics of Modernism* (London: Verso, 1989); T. J. Clark, *The Painting of Modern Life: Paris in the Art of Manet and His Followers* (London: Thames and Hudson, 1985); Christopher Prendergast, *Paris and the Nineteenth Century* (Oxford: Blackwell, 1992); Griselda Pollock, *Visions of Difference: Femininity, Feminism and the Histories of Art* (London: Routledge, 1989); Janet Wolff, 'The invisible flâneuse', *Theory, Culture and Society* 2:3 (1985), 37–48; Adrian Rifkin, *Street Noises: Parisian Pleasure 1900–1940* (Manchester: Manchester University Press, 1993).
11. Nigel Thrift, '"Not a straight line but curve", or, Cities are not mirrors of modernity', in David Bell and Azzedine Haddour (eds.), *City Visions* (Harlow: Longman, 2000), 245.
12. Malcolm Bradbury and James McFarlane, *Modernism 1890–1930* (London: Penguin, 1991), 13.
13. Jo Labanyi, 'Ghosts of Modernity', The Sir Henry Thomas Lecture Series, November 1, 2001, University of Birmingham.
14. Carlos Seco Serrano, *Sociedad, literatura y politica en la España del siglo XIX* (Madrid: Guadiana de Publicaciones, 1973), 196.
15. Michael Ugarte, *Madrid 1900: The Capital as Cradle of Literature and Culture* (Pennsylvania: The Pennsylvania State University Press, 1996).

16. Santos Juliá, David Ringrose and Cristina Segura, *Madrid: Historia de una capital* (Madrid: Alianza Editorial, 1994), 317.
17. Ramón María del Valle-Inclán, *Luces de bohemia*, trans. Antony N. Zahareas and Gerald Gillespie (Edinburgh: Edinburgh University Press, 1976), 183.
18. Marshall Berman, *All That is Solid Melts Into Air: The Experience of Modernity* (London: Penguin, 1982).
19. Ibid., 231–2.
20. Ibid., 232.
21. Saskia Sassen, *Cities in a World Economy* (London: Pine Forge Press, 1994).
22. David Ley, 'Modernism, post-modernism and the struggle for place', in J. Agnew and J. Duncan (eds.), *The Power of Place* (Boston: Unwin Hyman, 1989), 53; Henri Lefebvre, *Writings on Cities* (Oxford: Blackwell, 1996).
23. Ash Amin and Nigel Thrify, *Cities: Reimagining the Urban* (Cambridge: Polity, 2002); James Donald, *Imagining the Modern City* (London: Athlone, 1999).
24. Walter Benjamin and Asja Lacis, 'Naples', in *One-Way Street and Other Writings* (London: Verso, 1979), 167–76.
25. Walter Benjamin, *The Correspondence of Walter Benjamin*, ed. Gershom Scholem and Theodor Adorno, trans. Manfred Jacobson and Evelyn Jacobson (Chicago: University of Chicago Press, 1994), 253.
26. Ibid., 254.
27. Henri Lefebvre and Catherine Régulier, 'Rhythmanalysis of Mediterranean Cities', in *Writings on Cities*, 228.
28. John A. Agnew, 'The Devaluation of Place in Social Science', in Agnew and Duncan, 9–29, 19.
29. The appropriation of *lo castizo* by members of the Spanish intellectual movement known as the 'Generation of 1898', for whose anti-modern ideology it came to refer not so much to urban Madrid as to a myth of rural, peasant Castile, and the subsequent incorporation of this reading into the Franco regime's rhetoric of nationalist racial purity, has resulted in a tendency to neglect its *madrileño* connotations. Apart from when discussing this bowdlerization, I use the term throughout this study in its early nineteenth-century sense of localised urbanity and social ethnic marginality, in contrast to its Francoist construction as 'authentic' Spanishness. See also my account of the differing representation of *castizo* stereotypes under the Second Republic and under the Franco regime in Jo Labanyi (ed), *Constructing Identity in Contemporary Spain: Theoretical Debates and Cultural Practice* (Oxford: Oxford University Press, 2002), 178–205.
30. Berman, 17.
31. Paul Julian Smith, *The Moderns: Time, Space, and Subjectivity in Contemporary Spanish Culture* (Oxford: Oxford University Press, 2000)
32. Botton, 116.

Chapter 2 Madrid, 'Villa y Corte'

1. The domination of the Court within the city was comprehensibly demonstrated when Philip III's favourite, the Duque de Lerma, attempted to move it to Valladolid in 1601. By 1605 the population of Madrid had fallen to 26,000. When the Court returned in 1606, it immediately leaped back to 70,000.
2. Priscilla Parkhurst Ferguson, *Paris as Revolution: Writing the Nineteenth-Century City* (Berkeley: University of California Press, 1994).
3. Ramón Mesonero Romanos, *Manual de Madrid. Descripciones de la Villa y Corte . . .* (Madrid: D. M. de Burgos, 1831).
4. Ibid., 3.
5. Ramón Mesonero Romanos, *Apéndice al Manual de Madrid. Descripción de la corte y de la villa* (Madrid: Tomás Jordán, 1835)
6. In the same year he initiated and collaborated in the creation of the Ateneo, Madrid's philosophical, scientific and literary society.
7. Ramón Mesonero Romanos, *Manual de Madrid*, (Madrid: D. Antonio Yenes, 1844), 4.
8. Ford, *Gatherings from Spain* 264.
9. Ibid., 302.
10. Théophile Gautier, *Voyage en Espagne* (Paris: Julliard, 1964), quoted in Elizabeth Nash, *Madrid* (Oxford: Signal, 2001), 19.
11. Quoted in Michael Collie, *George Borrow Eccentric* (Cambridge: Cambridge University Press, 1982), 60.
12. George Borrow, *The Bible in Spain* (Philadelphia: Campbell, 1843), 59.
13. Quoted in Nash, 124.
14. Carlo M. Cipolla, *Literacy and Development in the West* (Harmondsworth: Penguin, 1969), 128.
15. Ramón Mesonero Romanos, *Panorama matritense* (Madrid: Imprenta Repullés, 1835).
16. Mesonero Romanos described the literature of *costumbrismo* in relation to these English and French writers in 'Retrato del autor', *Revista Española*, November 10, 1882, 13–14.
17. Ramón Mesonero Romanos, quoted in Publio López Mondéjar, *Madrid: Laberinto de memorias* (Madrid: Lunwerg, 1999), 39.
18. Jonathon Crary, *Techniques of the Observer: On Vision and Modernity in the Nineteenth Century* (Cambridge, Mass.: MIT Press, 1990).
19. Mariano José de Larra, *Articulos Completos* (Madrid: Aguilar, 1961), 197–207.
20. Ford, 256.
21. See, for example, Correa Calderón, *Costumbristas españoles* (Madrid: Aguilar, 1950).

22. Francisco Umbral, *Larra: anatomia de un dandy* (Madrid: Biblioteca Nueva, 1976), 117.
23. Ramón Mesonero Romanos, 'La Capa Vieja y El Baile de Candil', reprinted in M. Sanchez de Palacios, *Mesonero Romanos* (Madrid: Compañia Bibliografica Española, 1963), 103–8, 105.
24. Walter Benjamin, 'Paris – the Capital of the Nineteenth Century', in *Charles Baudelaire* trans. Harry Zohn (London: Verso, 1973), 161.
25. Ramón Mesonero Romanos, *Memorias de un setentón*, ed. José Escobar and Joaquín Álvarez Barrientos (Madrid: Editorial Catalia, 1994), 527.
26. Ibid., 529.
27. Ibid.
28. Escobar and Álvarez Barrientos, in Mesonero Romanos, *Memorias*, 38.
29. Ramón Mesonero Romanos, quoted in Publio López Mondéjar, *Madrid, Laberinto de memorias: cien años de fotografia, 1839–1936* (Barcelona: Lunwerg, 1999), 38.
30. Iain Chambers, *Migrancy, Culture, Identity* (London: Routledge, 1993), 92.
31. Escobar and Álvarez Barrientos, in Mesonero Romanos, *Memorias*, 30.
32. Ramón Mesonero Romanos, *Obras jocosas y satíricas del Curioso Parlante. Vol.1, Tipos, grupos y bocetas* (Madrid: Mellado, 1862), 14.
33. Ibid.
34. Ibid.
35. Ramón Mesonero Romanos, 'El Nuevo Madrid', reprinted in Sanchez de Palacios, 62–4, 64.
36. Benjamin, 161.
37. Mesonero Romanos, *Memorias*, 87.
38. Maria Balshaw and Liam Kennedy, *Urban Space and Representation* (London: Pluto, 2000).

Chapter 3 The Nineteenth-Century Capital

1. Quoted in William Shoemaker, *Los artículos de Galdós en 'La Nacion'* (Madrid: Insula, 1972), 189–90.
2. Benito Pérez Galdós, 'Some Observations on the Contemporary Novel in Spain', translated and reprinted in Jo Labanyi (ed.), *Galdós* (London: Longman, 1993), 32–3.
3. Ibid.
4. The Castro plan enlarged the city from 800 to over 2,200 hectares. Javier García Gutierrez-Mosterio, 'La ciudad en transición', in Virgilio Pinto Crespo,

Madrid: Atlas Historico de la Ciudad 1850–1939 (Madrid: Lunwerg, 2001), 64.

5. Luis Alfonso, quoted in Benito Pérez Galdós, *That Bringas Woman* ed. and trans. Catherine Jagoe (London: Everyman, 1996), 199.
6. Translated and reprinted in Jo Labanyi (ed.), *Galdós* (London: Longman, 1993), 46.
7. Diane Beth Hyman, 'The *Fortunata y Jacinta* Manuscript of Benito Pérez Galdós', Ph.D. Dissertation, Harvard University, 1972, 56.
8. Quoted in Hugh Thomas, *Madrid: A Traveller's Companion* (London: Constable, 1988).
9. Rafael Gil and Tomás Romea, *Guía de Madrid, 1881* (Madrid: Imprenta de Fortanet, 1881), 53.
10. Eduardo Alaminos and Eduardo Salas, 'Ocio y diversiones madrileños', in Pinto Crespo, *Madrid*, 363.
11. Lou Charnon-Deutsch, *Fictions of the Feminine in the Nineteenth-Century Spanish Press* (Pennsylvania: The Pennsylvania University Press, 2000), 133.
12. Geoffrey Crossick and Serge Jaumain, 'The world of the department store: distribution, culture and social change', in Crossick and Jaumain (eds.), *Cathedrals of Consumption: The European Department Store 1850–1939* (Ashgate: Aldershot, Hants, 1999), 10.
13. Rachel Bowlby, *Just Looking* (London: Methuen, 1985), 32.
14. Charnon-Deutsch, 135.
15. Mesonero Romanos, *Manual*, 451.
16. Ibid., 450.
17. Gil and Romea, *Guía*, 229. Developing later than in France, England and the United States, the nineteenth-century department store in Spain had little time to develop and consolidate its status before the economic slump of the 1890s, and the arrival of the low-cost, highly competitive *prix uniques*, stores that were less luxurious yet provided a large range of standard goods at a range of set, cheap prices.
18. Philippe Hamon, *Expositions: Literature and Architecture in Nineteenth-Century France*, translated by Katia Sainson-Frank and Lisa Maguire (Berkeley: University of California Press, 1992), 73.
19. *La Ilustración de España*, 22 May 1886, quoted in Carmen Ariza Muñoz, *Los Jardines del Buen Retiro* (Madrid: Lunwerg, 1989), 153.
20. Shoemaker, 89.
21. Ibid., 78.
22. Ibid.
23. Pío Baroja, *Las noches del Buen Retiro*, in *Obras Completas* vol. VI (Madrid: Biblioteca Nueva, 1948), 588.
24. Ibid., 589.

25. The Jardines del Buen Retiro were eventually destroyed in 1904 for the construction of the Palacio de Comunicaciones, the city's literally palatial post office. Their disappearance brought an end to the era of the Madrilenian pleasure park, constantly threatened by the eastern expansion of the city, and from the turn-of-the-century by the burgeoning dominance of the cinematograph.
26. Baroja, *Camino de perfección*, OC VI, 13.
27. Bowlby, *Just Looking*, 12.
28. Elizabeth Kowaleski-Wallace, *Consuming Subjects: Women, Shopping, and Business in the Eighteenth Century* (New York: Columbia University Press, 1997), 13.
29. Andreas Huyssen, *After the Great Divide: Modernism, Mass Culture and Postmodernism* (Basingstoke: Macmillan, 1986), 47.
30. 30. Ibid., 55.

Chapter 4 City of Contrasts

1. Vicente Blasco Ibáñez, *La horda* (1905).
2. Gili Ruiz and Velasco Medina, in Pinto Crespo, *Madrid*, 398.
3. Ibid., 400.
4. Philiph Hauser, *Madrid bajo el punto de vista médico-social* (Madrid, 1902); César Chicote, *Reorganización del servicio de la limpieza de Madrid* (Madrid, 1906). See also César Chicote, *La vivienda insalubre en Madrid* (Madrid: Imprenta Municipal, 1914).
5. Baroja, 'Crónica: Hampa', *El Pueblo Vasco*, 18 September 1903, collected in *Hojas sueltas*, 331–4.
6. Robert Park *et al* (eds), *The City* (Chicago: University of Chicago Press, 1967).
7. Carmen del Moral Ruiz, *La sociedad madrileña fin de siglo y Baroja* (Madrid: Ediciones Turner, 1974), 80.
8. Hauser, *Madrid*, 290.
9. George Eliot, 'The Natural History of German Life', in *Essays of George Eliot*, ed. Thomas Pinney (New York: Columbia University Press, 1963), 272.
10. Daniel Pick, *Faces of Degeneration* (Cambridge: Cambridge University Press, 1989), 21.
11. See Gil Maestre, *Los malhechores de Madrid* (Gerona, 1889) and Bernaldo de Quirós and José María Llanas Aguilaniedo, *La mala vida en Madrid* (Madrid: Rodríguez Serra, 1901).

12. Gregorio Marañon, *Contestación al discurso de don Pío Baroja en la Academia Española*, 12 May 1935, reprinted in F. Baeza, *Baroja y su mundo* (Madrid: Arion, 1961).
13. Peter Stallybrass and Allon White, *The Politics and Poetics of Trasngression* (Cornell: Cornell University Press, 1986), 3.
14. Mary Douglas, *Purity and Danger* (1966), 48.
15. Pío Baroja, 'El labrador y el vagabundo', OC vol. V, 53
16. Pío Baroja, 'Patología del golfo', Ibid., 55.
17. Hauser, *Madrid*, 210.
18. Benjamin, *Charles Baudelaire*, 19–20.
19. Emilia Pardo Bazán, 'En el tranvía', *Cuentos* (Madrid: Taurus, 1985), 101.
20. Ibid., 101.
21. Emilia Pardo Bazán, 'Castaways', *Torn Lace and Other Stories*, ed. and trans. Maria Cristina Urruela and Joyce Tolliver (New York: Modern Language Association, 1996), 109.
22. Ibid.
23. Peter Stallybrass and Allon White, *Transgression*, 191.
24. Vicente Juan Morant, 'Aproximacion a la arquitectura de los teatros madrileños de los siglos XVIII y XIX', in Museo Municipal de Madrid (ed.), *Cuatro Siglos de Teatro en Madrid* (Madrid: Museo Muncipal de Madrid, 1992), 53–67, 59.
25. Mª Encina Cortizo and Ramón Sobrino, 'La música en Madrid entre 1848–1939', in Pinto Crespo, *Madrid*, 373.
26. The *sainete* originated as a comical interlude between the second and third acts of longer productions, developing into a genre of popular theatre in its own right in the latter half of the eighteenth century with the works of Ramón de la Cruz. Dedicated to the expression and celebration of the types and customs of the common people of the city, the *sainete* immortalised a vision of Madrilenian folkloric and popular culture that would be taken up by both literary *costumbrismo* and the *género chico*. See Douglas R. McKay, *Carlos Arniches* (New York: Twayne, 1972), 39–42.
27. Jose Lopez Ruiz, *Historia del Teatro Apolo y de La verbena de la paloma* (Madrid: Avapiés, 1994).
28. F. Vela, 'El género chico', *Revista de Occidente*, 10 (1964), 364–9, 368.
29. Nancy J. Membrez, 'La (re)invención de Madrid en el teatro por horas: tipomanía y lenguaje', in Juan A. Ríos Carratalá (ed.), *Estudios sobre Carlos Arniches* (Alicante: Instituto de Cultura "Juan Gil-Albert", 1994), 75–89, 77.
30. Julio Caro Baroja, *Temas Castizos* (Madrid: Ediciones Istmo, 1980), 11. I wish again to distinguish my use of *lo castizo* in its original pre-Franco context, in contrast to the Nationalist and nostalgic construction of 'authentic' Spain that actually represses the ethnic, racial and class marginality with which *castizo*

originates. I refer to Caro Baroja's definition here because it emphasises the use of the term in relation to popular rather than national culture.

31. Conceptually similar to the English term 'cockney', both 'majo' and 'chulo' have almost identical meanings, designating an attractive, charming, perhaps rascally person, and most typically used in reference to the typical working-class Madrilenian. 'Majo', however, assumes the historical connotation of the eighteenth or early nineteenth century.

32. Stallybrass and White, *Transgression*, 177–8.

33. In *La fiesta de San Antón* the scene is almost identical, yet includes a carriage rank, at the back of which stands the last operative 'simón', a type of cab common in the city during the early and mid nineteenth century.

34. Carlos Arniches, 'El santo de la Isidra', in *Teatro Completo*, vol.1. (Madrid: Aguilar, 1948), 147.

35. P. Lozano Guirao, *Vida y obras de Ricardo de la Vega* (Madrid: Facultad de Filosofía y Letras, 1959), 12.

36. Carlos Arniches, *ABC*, 14 April 1917, quoted in Membrez, 85.

37. Quoted in Membrez, 86.

38. Vicente Blasco Ibáñez, 'El poeta de Madrid', in López Silva, *Gente de tufos* (Madrid: Lib. De Fernando Fe, 1905), 13.

39. See María Pilar Espín Templado, *El teatro por horas en Madrid (1870–1910)* (Madrid: Instituto de Estudios Madrileños, 1995), 139.

40. Felipe Pérez y González, *La Gran Vía* (1886), reprinted in *La Zarzuela Chica Madrileña: La Gran Vía, La Verbena de la Paloma, Agua, Azucarillos y Aguardiente, La Revoltosa*, ed. Fernando Doménech Rico (Madrid: Editorial Castalia, 1998), 116.

41. Pío Baroja, *La formación psicológica de un escritor*, Obras Completas V (Madrid: Biblioteca Nueva, 1948), 877.

42. Julio Caro Baroja, 'Prólogo', *La busca* (Madrid: Salvat Editores, 1982), 7–13, 9.

Chapter 5 Cosmpolitan Lights

1. David E. Nye, *Electrifying America: Social Meanings of a New Technology* (Cambridge, Mass.: MIT Press, 1990), 2.

2. Baroja, *Memorias*, 118

3. Wolfgang Schivelbusch, *Disenchanted Night: The Industrialisation of Light in the Nineteenth Century* (Oxford: Berg ,1988), 189.

4. Azorín, quoted in José M.ª Díez Borque, *Vistas literarias de Madrid entre siglos (xix – xx)* (Madrid: Comunidad de Madrid, 1998), 141.

5. J. Ortega Munilla, 'La villa sin calles', quoted in José Luis de Oriol, *Memoria del Proyecto de Reforma Interior de Madrid* (Madrid, 1921), 1.

6. See George Collins and Carlos Flores (eds.), *Arturo Soria y La Ciudad Lineal* (Madrid, 1968), for an anthology of writings by Soria.

7. Compañía Madrileño de Urbanización, *La Ciudad Lineal* (Madrid, 1894), quoted in Javier García Gutierrez-Mosterio, 'La ciudad de la Restauración', in Pinto Crespo, *Madrid*, 82.

8. Prices ranged from between 3,600 pesetas for the smallest, four-room dwellings, to 60,000 pesetas for a luxury villa onto the transport corridor.

9. Edward Baker, 'La Gran Vía entre el casticisimo y el cosmopolitanismo', in Pinto Crespo, *Madrid*, 131.

10. Quoted in F. Loyer, *Paris Nineteenth Century: Architecture and Urbanism* (New York: Abeville Press, 1988), 8.

11. Baker, 132.

12. Ibid, 130.

13. Similar to the magic lantern, the Edison kinetoscope was enclosed in a wooden case about four feet high, and presented a rapid succession of images on celluloid film that could be viewed through a single eyepiece in the top of the case. For an excellent discussion of the origins and various inventors of the moving picture, see Deac Rossell, *Living Pictures: The Origins of the Movies* (Albany: State University of New York Press, 1998).

14. Alaminos and Salas, 349–51.

15. *El País*, 19 June 1896. Quoted in Fernando López Serrano, *Madrid, figuras y sombras* (Madrid: Editorial Complutense, 1999), 83.

16. Ernesto Giménez Caballero, editor of *La Gaceta*, championed cinema as an art form, employing Luis Buñuel to direct its cinema section, and founding Madrid's radical film club, the Cineclub Español, in 1928, of which Pío Baroja and Ramón Gómez de la Serna were both members. See C. B. Morris, *This Loving Darkness: The Cinema and Spanish Writers 1920–1936* (Oxford: Oxford University Press, 1980) and Ramón Gubern, *Proyector de luna: La generación del 27 y el cine* (Barcelona: Anagrama, 1999) for excellent discussions of the influence of cinema on Spanish writers in the 1920s and 1930s.

17. Quoted in Morris, *Loving Darkness*, 30.

18. 'Del cinema a la fotografía. El nuevo arte de la cámara o la fotografía animista', LUZ (Madrid 2-1-1934), quoted in Hermeroteca Municipal de Madrid, *Revistas de Cine* (Madrid: Hermeroteca Municipal de Madrid, 1998), 70.

19. Morris, 34.

20. Alejandro Sawa, *Iluminaciones en la sombra* ed. Iris Zavala (Madrid: Alhambra, 1967), 80.

21. Quoted in López Serrano, 110–11.
22. Quoted and translated in Morris, 26.
23. Siegfried Kracauer, *The Mass Ornament* ed. Thomas Levin (Cambridge, Mass.: Harvard University Press, 1995), 323.
24. Ibid., 328.
25. Miriam Hansen, *Babel and Babylon: Spectatorship in American Silent Film* (Cambridge, Mass.: Harvard University Press, 1991), 245.
26. Ibid., 141.

Chapter 6 Urban Cosmorama

1. Ramón Gómez de la Serna, *Automoribundia 1888–1948*, vol. 1 (Madrid: Guadarama, 1974), 284.
2. Ramón Gómez de la Serna and Lawrence Smith, *Maruja Mallo 1928–1942* (Buenos Aires: Editorial Losada, 1942), 16. Young, beautiful, strikingly dressed, sexually liberated and notoriously linked with a number of male intellectuals of the Madrid scene (including Pablo Neruda and Rafael Alberti), Mallo was often exoticised as the *femme-enfant* of the Madrid avant-garde in this way.
3. For full biographical details see Juan Pérez de Ayala and Francisco Rivas (eds), *Maruja Mallo* (Madrid: Guillerma de Osma Galería, 1992).
4. Paloma Ulacia Altolaguirre and Concha Méndez, *Memorias habladas, memorias armadas* (Madrid: Mondadori, 1990), 58.
5. Quoted in Pérez de Ayala and Rivas, *Maruja Mallo*, 80.
6. Ibid., 78
7. Maruja Mallo, 'The Popular in Spanish Art', reprinted in Gómez de la Serna and Lawrence, 44.
8. Gómez de la Serna and Lawrence, 21.
9. Mallo, 44.
10. Ibid.
11. Ibid., 45.
12. Ibid.
13. Julio Payro, in *La Nación* (Buenos Aires), 29 May 1938, reprinted in Gómez de la Serna and Lawrence, 55.
14. Quoted in Shirley Mangini, *Las modernas de Madrid: Las grandes intelectuales españolas de la vanguardia* (Barcelona: Península, 2001), 124.
15. See Román Gubern, *Benito Perojo: pionerismo y supervivencia* (Madrid: Filmoteca Española, 1994).

16. Antonio Barbero, Review of *La Verbena de la Paloma*, *ABC*, 24 December 1935.
17. See Mikhail Bakhtin, *Rabelais and his World*, trans. Helene Iswolsky (Bloomington, Ind.: Indiana University Press, 1984).
18. Michael Holquist, 'Prologue', in Bakhtin, xviii.
19. Mallo, 44.
20. Derek Harris, *The Spanish Avant-Garde* (Manchester: Manchester University press, 1995), 3–4.
21. Pablo Neruda, 'RAMON', in Ramón Gómez de la Serna, *Obras selectas* (Barcelona, 1971), 8; Octavio Paz, 'Una de cal . . .', *Papeles de Son Armadans*, 140 (1967), 186–7.
22. José Ortega y Gasset, *La deshumanización del arte* (Madrid: Espasa-Calpe, 1987), 76.
23. Quoted in Rita Mazzetti Gardiol, *Ramón Gómez de la Serna* (New York: Twayne, 1974), 130.
24. Keith Tester (ed.), *The Flâneur* (London: Routledge, 1994), 6–7.
25. Quoted in Gardiol, 130.
26. Ramón Gómez de la Serna, *Guia del Rastro* (Madrid: Taurus, 1961), 9.
27. Ibid., 11.
28. Ibid., 15.
29. Walter Benjamin, *The Arcades Project* trans. Howard Eiland and Kevin McLaughlin (Cambridge, Mass.; Harvard University Press, 1999), 205.
30. Jorge Luis Borges, quoted in Andrés Soria Olmedo, 'Ramón Gómez de la Serna's Oxymoronic Historiography of the Avant-Garde', in Harris, 15–26, 19.
31. Ramón Gómez de la Serna, *Las tres gracias* (Madrid: Perseo, 1949), 12.
32. Francisco Umbral, *Ramón y las vanguardias* (Madrid: Espasa-Calpe, 1978), 132
33. Francisco Umbral, *Spleen de Madrid* (Madrid: Sala, 1972), 120.

Chapter 7 Epilogue

1. Camilo José Cela, *The Hive*, trans. J. M. Cohen and Arturo Barea (Illinois: Dalkey Archive Press, 2001), 167.
2. Smith, *The Moderns*, 9.
3. Pedro Almodóvar, 'The Vocation', in Almodóvar, 132.
4. Manuel Castells, *The City and the Grassroots: A Cross-Cultural Theory of Urban Social Movements* (London: Edward Arnold, 1983).

5. Ibid., 217.
6. Ibid., xvi.
7. Ibid., 216.
8. Almodóvar, 'Coming to Madrid' in Almodóvar, 91–2
9. Smith, 6.
10. Almodóvar, ix.
11. Pedro Almodóvar, 'Promotion', in Almodóvar, 125
12. Almodóvar, 'Coming to Madrid' in Almodóvar, 92.
13. Quoted in Mark Allinson, *The Films of Pedro Almodóvar* (London: I. B. Tauris, 2001), 111.

Select Bibliography

Almodóvar, Pedro (1992), *The Patty Diphusa Stories*, trans. Kirk Anderson (London: Faber and Faber, 1992)

Altolaguirre, Paloma Ulacia and Concha Méndez (1990), *Memorias habladas, memorias armadas* (Madrid: Mondadori)

Amorós, Andrés (1991), *Luces de candilejas: los espectáculos en España 1898–1939* (Madrid: Espasa Calpe)

Arniches, Carlos (1948), *Teatro Completo* (Madrid: Aguilar)

Baeza, F. (1961), *Baroja y su mundo* (Madrid: Arion)

Bahamonde Magro, A. and J. Toro Mérida (1978), *Burguesia, especulacion y cuestion social en el Madrid del siglo XIX* (Madrid: Siglo XXI)

Bakhtin, Mikhail (1984), *Rabelais and his World*, trans. Hélène Iswolsky (Bloomington, Ind.: Indiana University Press)

Barbero, Antonio (1935), Review of *La Verbena de la Paloma*, *ABC*, 24 December.

Baroja, Pío (1948), *Obras Completas* (Madrid: Biblioteca Nueva)

Bell, David and Azzedine Haddour (eds.) (2000), *City Visions* (Harlow: Longman)

Benjamin, Walter (1979), *One-Way Street and Other Writings*, trans. Edmund Jephcott and Kingsley Shorter (London: Verso)

—— (1999), *The Arcades Project* trans. Howard Eiland and Kevin McLaughlin (Cambridge, Mass.; Harvard University Press)

Berman, Marshall (1982), *All That is Solid Melts Into Air: The Experience of Modernity* (London: Penguin)

Bowlby, Rachel (1985), *Just Looking* (London: Methuen)

Bradbury, Malcolm and James McFarlane (1991), *Modernism 1890–1930* (London: Penguin, 1991)

Caro Baroja, Julio (1980), *Temas Castizos* (Madrid: Ediciones Istmo)

Carr, Raymond (1980), *Modern Spain 1875–1980* (Oxford: Oxford University Press)

Castells, Manuel (1983), *The City and the Grassroots: A Cross-Cultural Theory of Urban Social Movements* (London: Edward Arnold)

—— (2002), *The Castells Reader on Cities and Social Theory* ed. Ida Susser (Oxford: Blackwell)

Chambers, Iain (1993), *Migrancy, Culture, Identity* (London: Routledge)

Charnon-Deutsch, Lou (1999), *Fictions of the Feminine in the Nineteenth-Century Spanish Press* (Pennsylvania: The Pennsylvania University Press)

Círculo de Bellas Artes (1993), *Carnavales* (Madrid: Círculo de Bellas Artes)

Clarke, T. J. (1985), *The Painting of Modern Life: Paris in the Art of Manet and his Followers* (London: Thames and Hudson)

Collins, George and Carlos Flores (eds.) (1968), *Arturo Soria y La Ciudad Lineal* (Madrid)

Crary, Jonathon (1990), *Techniques of the Observer: On Vision and Modernity in the Nineteenth Century* (Cambridge, Mass.: MIT Press)

Crossick, Geoffrey and Serge Jaumain (eds.) (1999), *Cathedrals of Consumption: The European Department Store 1850–1939* (Ashgate: Aldershot, Hants)

De Botton, Alain (2002), *The Art of Travel* (London: Hamish Hamilton)

Doane, Mary Ann (1987), *The Desire to Desire: The Woman's Film of the 1940s* (Bloomington: Indiana University Press)

Doménech Rico, Fernando (ed.) (1998), *La Zarzuela Chica Madrileña: La Gran Vía, La Verbena de la Paloma, Agua, Azucarillos y Aguardiente, La Revoltosa* (Madrid: Editorial Castalia)

Espín Templado, María Pilar (1995), *El teatro por horas en Madrid (1870–1910)* (Madrid: Instituto de Estudios Madrileños)

Ford, Richard (2000), *Gatherings from Spain* ed. Ian Robertson (London: Pallas Athene)

Frisby, David (2001), *Cityscapes of Modernity* (London: Polity)

García Rodero, Cristina (1992), *Festivals and Rituals of Spain* (New York: Harry N. Abrams)

Gil, Rafael and Tomás Romea (1881), *Guía de Madrid, 1881* (Madrid: Imprenta de Fortanet)

Gilmore, David (1998), *Carnival and Culture: Sex, Symbol, and Status in Spain* (New Haven: Yale University Press)

Gómez de la Serna, Ramón (1949), *Las tres gracias* (Madrid: Perseo)

—— (1961), *Guia del Rastro* (Madrid: Taurus)

—— (1974), *Automoribundia 1888–1948*, vol. 1 (Madrid: Guadarama)

—— (1995), *Cinelandia*, (Madrid: Valdemar)

—— (1998), *Historia del Puerta del Sol* (Madrid: Almarubu)

—— and Lawrence Smith (1942), *Maruja Mallo 1928–1942* (Buenos Aires: Editorial Losada)

Gubern, Román (1994), *Benito Perojo: pionerismo y supervivencia* (Madrid: Filmoteca Española)

—— (1999), *Proyector de luna: La generación del 27 y el cine* (Barcelona: Anagrama)

Gutiérrez Solana, José (1995), *Madrid Callejero* (Madrid: Editorial Castalia)

Hansen, Miriam (1991), *Babel and Babylon: Spectatorship in American Silent Film* (Cambridge, Mass.: Harvard University Press)

—— (1999), 'The mass production of the senses: classical cinema as vernacular modernism', *Modernism / modernity* 6:2, 59–77

Hermeroteca Municipal de Madrid (1998), *Revistas de Cine* (Madrid: Hermeroteca Municipal de Madrid)

Huyssen, Andreas (1986), *After the Great Divide: Modernism, Mass Culture and Postmodernism* (Basingstoke: Macmillan)

Jacobs, Michael (1992), *Madrid Observed* (London, Pallas Athene)

Juliá, Santos, Ringrose, David and Cristina Segura (1994), *Madrid: Historia de una capital* (Madrid: Alianza Editorial)

Kany, C. E. (1930), *Fiestas y costumbres españolas* (London: Harrap)

Kracauer, Siegfried (1995), *The Mass Ornament* ed. Thomas Levin (Cambridge, Mass.: Harvard University Press)

Kowaleski-Wallace, Elizabeth (1997), *Consuming Subjects: Women, Shopping, and Business in the Eighteenth Century* (New York: Columbia University Press)

Labanyi, Jo (ed.) (1993), *Galdós* (London: Longman)

—— (1997), 'Race, Gender and Disavowal in Spanish cinema of the early Franco period: the missionary film and the folkloric musical', *Screen* 38:3, pp. 215–31.

—— (ed.) (2002), *Constructing Identity in Contemporary Spain: Theoretical Debates and Cultural Practice* (Oxford: Oxford University Press)

Lacarta, Manuel (1986), *Madrid y sus literaturas: de la generación del 98 a la postguerra* (Madrid: Avapiés)

Lefebvre, Henri (1996), *Writings on Cities* (Oxford: Blackwell)

López Mondéjar, Publio (1999), *Madrid: Laberinto de memorias* (Madrid: Lunwerg)

Lopez Ruiz, José (1994), *Historia del Teatro Apolo y de La verbena de la paloma* (Madrid: Avapiés)

Loyer, F. (1988), *Paris Nineteenth Century: Architecture and Urbanism* (New York: Abeville Press)

Lozano Guirao, P. (1959), *Vida y obras de Ricardo de la Vega* (Madrid: Facultad de Filosofía y Letras)

Mangini, Shirley (2001), *Las modernas de Madrid: Las grandes intelectuales españolas de la vanguardia* (Barcelona: Península)

Mazzetti Gardiol, Rita (1974), *Ramón Gómez de la Serna* (New York: Twayne)

McKay, Douglas R. (1972), *Carlos Arniches* (New York: Twayne)

Mellen, Joan (ed.) (1978), *The World of Luis Buñuel* (New York: Oxford University Press)

Merino, Antonio Guzmán (1935), Review of *La Verbena de la Paloma*, *Cinegramas* 68, 29 December

Mesonero Romanos, Ramón (1844), *Manual de Madrid*, (Madrid: D. Antonio Yenes)

—— (1945), *Escenas Matritenses* (Madrid: Aguilar)

—— (1994), *Memorias de un setentón* (Madrid: Editorial Castalia)

Mintz, Jerome (1997), *Carnival Song and Society* (Oxford: Berg)

Moral Ruiz, Camern del (1974), *La sociedad madrileña fin de siglo y Baroja* (Madrid: Ediciones Turner)

Morris, C. B. (1980), *This Loving Darkness: The Cinema and Spanish Writers 1920–1936* (Oxford: Oxford University Press)

Morton, H. V. (2002), *A Stranger in Spain* (London: Methuen)

Morus, Iwan Rhys (1998), *Frankenstein's Children: Electricity, Exhibition and Experiment in Early-Nineteenth-Century London* (Princeton, NJ.: Princeton University Press)

Museo Municipal de Madrid (1991), *Carteles de Fiestas en la Coleccion del Museo Municipal 1932–1991* (Madrid: Ayuntamiento de Madrid)

—— (ed.) (1992), *Cuatro Siglos de Teatro en Madrid* (Madrid: Museo Muncipal de Madrid)

Nash, Elizabeth (2001), *Madrid* (Oxford: Signal)

Nye, David E. (1990), *Electrifying America: Social Meanings of a New Technology* (Cambridge, Mass.: MIT Press)

Ortega y Gasset, José (1987), *La deshumanización del arte* (Madrid: Espasa-Calpe)

Pardo Bazán, Emilia (1985), *Cuentos* (Madrid: Taurus)

—— (1996), *Torn Lace and Other Stories*, ed. and trans. Maria Cristina Urruela and Joyce Tolliver (New York: Modern Language Association)

Parkhurst Ferguson, Priscilla (1994), *Paris as Revolution: Writing the Nineteenth-Century City* (Berkeley: University of California Press)

Payne, Stanley G. (1993), *Spain's First Democracy: The Second Republic 1931–1936* (Madison, Wisconsin: University of Wisconsin Press)

Pérez de Ayala, Juan and Rivas, Francisco (1991), *Maruja Mallo* (Madrid: Guillermo de Osma Galería)

Pérez Galdós, Benito (1976), *The Disinherited*, ed. and trans. Lester Clark (London: Phoenix House)

—— (1986), *Fortunata y Jacinta*, ed. and trans. Agnes Moncy Gullón (London: Penguin)

—— (1996), *That Bringas Woman* ed. and trans. Catherine Jagoe (London: Everyman)

Pick, Daniel (1989), *Faces of Degeneration* (Cambridge: Cambridge University Press)

Pinney, Thomas (ed.) (1963), *Essays of George Eliot* (New York: Columbia University Press)

Pinto Crespo, Virgilio (ed) (2001), *Madrid: Atlas Historico de la Ciudad 1850–1939* (Madrid: Lunwerg)

Prendergast, Christopher (1992), *Paris and the Nineteenth Century* (Oxford: Blackwell)

Rifkin, Adrian (1993), *Street Noises: Parisian Pleasure 1900–40* (Manchester: Manchester University Press)

Ringrose, David (1996), *Spain, Europe, and the 'Spanish Miracle', 1700–1900* (Cambridge: Cambridge University Press)

Ríos Carratalá, Juan A. (ed.) (1994), *Estudios sobre Carlos Arniches* (Alicante: Instituto de Cultura)

Rossell, Deac (1998), *Living Pictures: The Origins of the Movies* (Albany: State University of New York Press)

Salaün, Serge and Serrano, Carlos (1991), *1900 en España* (Madrid: Espasa Calpe)

Sanchez de Palacios, M. (1963), *Mesonero Romanos* (Madrid: Compañia Bibliografica Española)

Sawa, Alejandro (1967), *Iluminaciones en la sombra* ed. Iris Zavala (Madrid: Alhambra)

Segel, Harold B. (1987), *Turn of the Century Cabaret: Paris, Barcelona, Berlin, Munich, Vienna, Cracow* (New York: Columbia University Press)

Serrano, Carlos (1973), *Sociedad, literatura y política en la España del siglo XIX* (Madrid: Guardiana de Publicaciones)

Schivelbuch, Wolfgang (1988), *Disenchanted Night: The Industrialisation of Light in the Nineteenth Century* (Oxford: Berg)

Sheppard, Richard (1983), 'Tricksters, carnival and the magical figures of Dada poetry', *Forum for Modern Language Studies* 19:2, 116–25

Shields, Rob (1999), *Lefebvre, Love and Struggle: Spatial Dialectics* (London: Routledge)

Shoemaker, William (1972), *Los artículos de Galdós en 'La Nacion'* (Madrid: Insula)

Smith, Paul Julian (2000), *The Moderns: Time, Space and Subjectivity in Contemporary Spanish Culture* (Oxford: Oxford University Press)

Stallybrass, Peter and Allon White (1986), *The Politics and Poetics of Transgression* (Cornell: Cornell University Press)

Talens, Jenaro and Zunzunegui, Santos (1998), *Modes of Representation in Spanish Cinema* (Minneapolis: University of Minnesota Press)

Tester, Keith (ed.) (1994), *The Flâneur* (London: Routledge)

Umbral, Francisco (1972), *Spleen de Madrid* (Madrid: Sala)

—— (1978), *Ramón y las vanguardias* (Madrid: Espasa-Calpe)

Valle-Inclán, Ramón del (1976), *Luces de Bohemia*, trans. Anthony Zahareas and Gerald Gillespie (Edinburgh: Edinburgh University Press)

Ward, David and Oliver Zunz (eds.) (1992), *The Landscape of Modernity* (New York: Russell Sage Foundation)

Index

Index

Index

Breinigsville, PA USA
15 February 2011
255637BV00003B/23/P